HOW TO BE
HEARD*in*
HEAVEN

Bethany House Publishers books
by Eddie Smith

Breaking the Enemy's Grip

How to Be Heard in Heaven

Strategic Prayer*

*with Michael Hennen

HOW TO BE
HEARD *in*
HEAVEN

EDDIE SMITH

BETHANYHOUSE
Minneapolis, Minnesota

Published by Bethany House Publishers
11400 Hampshire Avenue South
Bloomington, Minnesota 55438

Bethany House Publishers is a division of
Baker Publishing Group, Grand Rapids, Michigan.

Printed in the United States of America

ISBN-13:   978-0-7642-0392-3
ISBN-10:   0-7642-0392-4

Library of Congress Cataloging-in-Publication Data

Smith, Eddie.
    How to be heard in heaven : moving from need-driven to God-centered prayer / Eddie Smith.
        p.   cm.
    Summary: "This practical book helps Christians understand how to pray more accurately, effectively, and realistically to achieve greater power, purpose, and passion in their spiritual lives. It shows readers who have felt ineffective in their prayer life how to mature in their prayer life"—Provided by publisher.
        ISBN-13: 978-0-7642-0392-3 (pbk. : alk. paper)
        ISBN-10: 0-7642-0392-4 (pbk. : alk. paper)
        1. Prayer—Christianity. I. Title.
    BV210.3.S64   2007
    248.3'2—dc22   2007009089

In keeping with biblical principles of creation stewardship, Baker Publishing Group advocates the responsible use of our natural resources. As a member of the Green Press Initiative, our company uses recycled paper when possible. The text paper of this book is comprised of 30% post-consumer waste.

green press INITIATIVE

This book is dedicated to Martha Day, whom I called my "mother-in-love." I preferred that designation over "mother-in-law." Martha, a delightful, godly lady, now awaits Alice's and my arrival in heaven. I still remember her sitting on our couch for two days intently reading this manuscript in its roughest form. How could she focus with all the traffic through the room and the television blaring? Then it dawned on me. She simply turned off her hearing aids to create the perfect reading environment. Seeing her so deeply engrossed in this book is my most cherished endorsement.

EDDIE SMITH, the cofounder and president of the U.S. Prayer Center, is a cross-denominational prayer leader and teacher, an internationally known conference speaker, and an author. Before founding the U.S. Prayer Center in 1990, Eddie and his wife, Alice, served sixteen years in itinerant evangelism and fourteen years in local churches. Eddie and Alice make their home in Houston, Texas.

CONTENTS

CONTENTS

INTRODUCTION

Most of us have resigned ourselves to the fact that voice mail is an irritating, yet necessary, part of our lives. Consider what it would be like if God installed voice mail on heaven's switchboard. Imagine praying and hearing the following:

Thank you for calling heaven.
> For English, press 1
> For Spanish, press 2
> For all other languages, press 3

Please select from one of the following:
> Press 1 for requests
> Press 2 for thanksgiving
> Press 3 for complaints
> Press 4 for all others

I am sorry; all of our angels are busy helping other people right now. However, your prayer is important to us, and we will answer it in the order it was received. Please stay on the line.

If you would like to speak to:
God the Father, press 1
Jesus, press 2
the Holy Spirit, press 3

To find a loved one who has been assigned to heaven, press 5, and then enter his or her Social Security number followed by the pound sign. If you receive a negative response, please hang up and dial area code 666.

For reservations to heaven, please enter J-O-H-N, followed by the numbers 3:16.

For answers to nagging questions about dinosaurs and life on other planets, please wait until you arrive in heaven.

The office is now closed for the weekend to observe a religious holiday.

If you are calling after hours and need emergency assistance, please contact your local pastor.

Thank you, and have a heavenly day.

—Author Unknown

Legendary radio news commentator Paul Harvey reports a true story about a stork in Florida that mated with another stork, then built her nest near a golf course.

She faithfully sat on her nest for weeks until naturalists discovered that she was sitting on a pile of golf balls—not eggs! It's fair to say that had she sat there for the rest of her life, she'd not have produced a thing.

Some folks feel like sincerity and consistency are the keys to answered prayer. I'm writing to suggest there is more to praying and being heard in heaven than sincerity and consistency.

Can we ever forget the annoying Verizon cell phone commercial that posed the burning question, "Can you hear me now?" However, when it comes to prayer, there isn't a more important question for us to ask. I'm sure you'll agree that *being heard* is infinitely more important than *praying*.

At any given moment, billions of people around the world are praying. How many do you suppose are speaking to the living God? More important, of those who are, how many do you think He hears? Obviously He will not answer a prayer He doesn't hear.

In Matthew 6:7, Jesus said of the heathen who babble repetitious prayers, "They think they shall be heard for their much speaking" (KJV), implying that they won't be heard. To spend one's entire life praying prayers that aren't heard in heaven is as fruitless as a stork trying to hatch a nest full of golf balls!

Certainly what we say in prayer is important, but we shouldn't forget that it's the *person,* not the *prayer,* that God hears. He doesn't answer prayer. God answers praying people. So in your quest to be heard in heaven, become a person God listens to.

One of my life goals is to be a person God hears. As my wife, Alice, points out in her bestselling book *Beyond the Veil,* God doesn't have favorites, but He does have intimates.

Crowds followed Jesus. The Twelve were His disciples, who walked with Him daily. However, Peter, James, and John were intimates of Jesus. And John is described as "the disciple Jesus loved." Or at least, that's how John saw it. (See John 13:23.)

That's my life goal. And my goal in writing this book is to convince you to make it your goal too!

PRINCIPLES *for* SUCCESSFUL PRAYER

WOULDN'T IT BE the best gift ever if I could present you with a formula that would guarantee that from now on, all your prayers would be answered? Nice, perhaps. But I can't. There is no magical prayer or magical form of prayer that God always answers affirmatively. "What about the prayer of Jabez?" some might ask. Well, think about it. If Jabez's prayer were a prayer with *a guaranteed answer,* Jesus would have instructed His disciples, saying, "Pray the prayer that Jabez prayed." Instead, He taught them to pray, "Our Father, who art in heaven. . . ." Further, if God *had* to answer our prayers, He would cease to be God. We would be gods, and He would be reduced to focusing on us, receiving our instructions, and serving up what we order. Sadly, if you listen to some people pray, that seems to be what they expect! Okay, let me be the first to confess. . . .

One day I was praying one of those oft-repeated parental prayers for one of our sons. I don't remember my exact words, but they were something like, "O God, fix my son. He's into this and into that. He needs this, and he needs that. God, how long must I pray before you move in his life?" With that the Holy Spirit abruptly interrupted me. He said, "Eddie, that's not prayer. You're slandering me."

Shocked and befuddled, I said, "Slandering you, Lord? What do you mean, I'm slandering you? You know I'd never do that."

God continued, "All right, allow me to interpret what you just prayed. First, you obviously think you know your son's needs, and although I created him, I don't have a clue. Secondly, it sounds as if you feel that you love your son, but I don't. Finally, you seem to be suggesting that if you were me, you'd already have done something, and I haven't. Doesn't that about cover it?"

I had to admit that He was right. After all, He's God! But I was at a loss as to *what I should pray*. So I waited.

After an uncomfortable moment or two, I heard prayer rising from my heart to His, unlike any I'd ever prayed before. It sounded like this.

> *Father, I thank you for loving me and for hearing my prayers. I praise you for the plan and purpose you have for my son—for you wrote the days of his life in your book before he was even born. I'm grateful to know that your plans are perfect, and your purposes never change. Thank you for assuring me in Philippians 1:6 that what you have begun in his life you are busy finishing. Thank you for changing his schedule and bringing people into his life that he never expected to meet. Thank you for reminding him*

of things his mother, Alice, and I have taught him since he was a small child. . . .

From that moment on, Alice and I began praying in a new way for our children. Six months later, our son called Alice and said, "Mother, I know you and Dad have prayed for me all my life. But you've changed the way you pray for me, haven't you?"

She said, "Yes, son, we have."

He continued, "It's been about six months, hasn't it?"

She acknowledged that it had been exactly six months. "But how do you know that?" she asked.

"Mother, until six months ago, I felt confused in my mind and condemned in my heart. But for the past six months I've felt clear-minded and drawn to God." Since then, we've watched God at work in our son's life, drawing him ever so slowly to himself.

Thank God, I'm not the only one God has ever interrupted while they were praying. God interrupted Joshua when he was praying for Israel, after their defeat at Ai. Joshua was facedown on the ground, covered in sackcloth and ashes. At least I hadn't gone that far! God said to Joshua (my paraphrase): "It's not time to pray. It's time for you to get up and clean house. You folks have hidden forbidden things among your stuff. Your army will never win another battle until you find and rid yourselves of those defiled things." (See Joshua 7:10–12.)

God also interrupted Moses and the children of Israel at the Red Sea, where they were trapped by Pharaoh and the world's greatest army. You might say they were "caught between the devil and the deep blue sea"; or, as we say in Texas, "between a rock and a hard place." They cried out (whined, actually) to God about their circumstance. What was God's response? He essentially said, "Folks, this is no time to pray. Moses, raise the rod and split the sea." And Moses did! (See Exodus 14:15–16.) Since He interrupted Joshua and Moses, I didn't feel too bad when He interrupted me. I felt like I was in pretty good company.

I don't promise to teach you how to *get what you want* from God. But I do hope that by the time you finish reading this book, you will know *how to be heard in heaven*. Why? Because your prayers will never be answered if they are never heard.

THREE PRAYING PEOPLE GOD WON'T HEAR

Oh, I know, some folks think God hears every prayer. But that's just not the case. I can think of at least three categories of people God refuses to listen to.

- First, God won't hear a person who *regards iniquity*. David the psalmist wrote, "If I regard iniquity in my heart, *the Lord will not hear*" (Psalm 66:18 NKJV, emphasis added). To regard iniquity is not synonymous with a failure to confess sin. If God can't hear us unless we've confessed every sin, then we'll never be heard. Why? Because at any given time we are aware of only a fraction of the sins we've committed. Like the psalmist David concluded, "Who can discern his errors? Forgive my hidden faults" (Psalm 19:12).

This verse about "regarding iniquity" is about *preferring sin*. When I tell someone, "Give my regards to your wife," I'm saying, "Tell her that I honor her." *The Message* version of

Psalm 66:18 brings it into focus. It says, "If I had been cozy with evil, the Lord would never have listened." The person who is heard in heaven isn't a person who doesn't sin. It's a person who doesn't *prefer* sin, isn't cozy with it, doesn't think fondly of it or honor it. He has the same opinion about sin that God has. He hates it, shuns it, and longs to be free from it. The most committed Christian among us will occasionally sin. But a person of integrity hates sin and quickly repents.

- The second type of person God refuses to hear is someone who *tries to manipulate Him* in prayer. Jesus told His disciples in Matthew 6:7 that the pagans thought they would be heard for their "much speaking." The implication was . . . they weren't!

Later in this book we'll consider other ways that people try to manipulate God in prayer. In most cases, they don't even know they are doing it. Paul said, "When I was a child, I talked like a child, I thought like a child, I reasoned like a child. When I became a man, I put childish ways behind me" (1 Corinthians 13:11). Growing requires becoming aware of certain things we are doing wrong and putting them away.

- Third, God won't hear the prayer of a "double-minded person." James tells us: "If any of you lacks wisdom, he should ask God, who gives generously to all without finding fault, and it will be given to him. But when he asks [prays], he must believe and not doubt, because he who doubts is like a wave of the sea, blown and tossed by the wind. *That man [or woman] should not think he will receive anything from the Lord*; he is a double-minded man, unstable in all he does" (James 1:5–8).

Here God promises *not to answer* the prayers of those who are double-minded. I'll discuss the importance of single-minded prayer later, but for now, I have some good news!

In every generation there have been those whom God *has* heard and answered. He hears the righteous, the expectant, and those who celebrate His responses. I hope as we walk through the pages of this book that your spiritual horizon expands, and that you'll receive a greater revelation of God's gracious offer to hear and answer you. As I write these words, I'm praying that you will see, perhaps for the first time, the unique position you have as a result of His death, burial, resurrection, ascension, and the coming of His Holy Spirit. Only then can you take full advantage and see miraculous things happen when you pray.

We're going to look at the remarkable contrast between the ways David and other Old Testament saints approached God and the way New Testament believers (especially after Pentecost) approached God—people like the apostle Paul. Our discoveries will broaden our understanding of prayer and give us a clearer perspective of who God is, who we are, and how we fit into His plan. When we begin to pray from the redemptive side of the cross, we'll begin to recognize the awesome opportunity that's ours as New Testament believers.

You'll have to agree that the wickedness of this world increases by the moment. The international dilemmas are staggering. Nations are beginning to recognize and admit their helplessness. Whether they know it or not, they are looking for a messiah.

The evil that lies in wait for our families is increasing exponentially. The *Ozzie and Harriet, Leave It to Beaver,* and *Father Knows Best* days are gone forever. Our ability to engage in effective prayer, prayer that God hears and delights to answer, is critical for the days ahead. We begin by looking at three levels of prayer.

THREE LEVELS OF PRAYER

Praying to Receive

The first level of prayer most of us experience is praying to receive.

Years ago I was conducting a revival meeting in Mississippi. One evening, following the service, we went to dinner at a beautiful old antebellum home that belonged to some church members.

While we were eating I noticed an odd chain that extended through the wall near the dining table. Mystified by it, I asked the homeowner what it was. He explained that it was a "servant's chain," from the days of slavery. When the slave owner's family was ready to be served their dinner, they summoned their servants by pulling the chain.

Prayer is often seen as a way for us to "pull God's chain," to persuade Him to meet our needs. We have a need, we pray, and God responds with an answer. Isn't that often our perception of prayer? This is the most elementary understanding and application of prayer, not unlike a hungry baby who cries for his food.

But there are other aspects of prayer that we grow to understand and experience.

Praying to Relate

Over time some of us may learn that prayer is more than "pulling God's chain" to get something from Him. We begin to see prayer as a way *to relate* to our heavenly Father. Prayer becomes an act of worship, an intimate spiritual relationship between a bride (us) and a groom (Christ). No other religion attempts to pray at this level. Their gods have no interest in a loving and personal relationship with them.

At this point we move beyond simply approaching God for things, even good and important things. In fact, our focus is no longer on ourselves at all. It is now on our "heavenly lover."

Some are so programmed toward serving God that they never discover this intimate aspect of prayer. They elevate what they do *for* God above relating intimately *to* Him.

When you enter this level of prayer you learn that it's not primarily about your needs being met. It's about meeting Christ's needs of worship, praise, and adoration. (See John 4:23.) But there's a third level of prayer. I believe it is the highest level.

Praying to Produce

God is beginning to reveal to us here at the beginning of the twenty-first century how prayer *to receive* blends with prayer *to relate* to become prayer *to produce!*

Consider for a moment a man and his wife who cannot produce children. From ancient times barrenness has been thought of as tragic. The childless couple has affection for and an attraction to each other. They are intimately engaged with each other. They find great personal fulfillment in their relationship. But they desire more. They want a child. They are programmed for reproduction. If they cannot produce children, they feel unfulfilled.

The same is true with prayer. Through prayer our basic needs are satisfied. We pray and God responds. Through prayer we experience intimacy with God. We exchange vows of love, we adore Him, and He adores us. But the ultimate purpose of our divine romance is to produce fruit. What kind of fruit? Every tree produces fruit after its kind. We are expected to produce *kingdom fruit* that will in time produce more *kingdom fruit*.

One day God's glorious kingdom will be fulfilled on this earth. Today, we can experience a "pre-fillment" of His kingdom in our hearts. We, the King's bride, in concert with Him, are to produce kingdom results to see the kingdom of God displace the kingdom of darkness through spiritual warfare. Through prayer we will soon see the kingdoms of this earth become the kingdoms of our God! Key to this is our being heard in heaven.

This book is about change. Writing it has changed me. Reading it will change you. If you, like me, are dissatisfied with the general ineffectiveness of your prayer life and want to step up to a new dimension with revelation that will unlock the heavenlies and release God's power, both in your own life and in the lives of those you love, then welcome aboard. Fasten your seat belt! You are the very person I've been waiting for.

There is a prayer protocol in heaven. It isn't complex, but it is very real. How we see and approach God is critical to our being heard by Him. It isn't true that He hears every prayer. We can and should learn how to present our cases in heaven's court in ways that increase the likelihood of our being heard and winning our petitions. I'm calling you to a place of spiritual maturity in prayer.

When Robert, our eldest son and current vice-president

of operations for our ministry, was four years old, he and I were sitting in a shoe store while his mom shopped for shoes. Like any four-year-old boy, he began to grow a bit restless. Frankly, so was I.

As he walked by me I said with a serious tone, "Son, when are you going to grow up?"

His big brown eyes rolled up and to the left as he grasped for a thought. He said, "I'm gonna do it right now."

With that, he rose to his tiptoes, threw back his tiny shoulders, gritted his teeth, and exerted all the effort he could muster to stretch himself taller. After a couple of fruitless and frustrating moments, a look of disappointment fell across his cherubic face. He said, "I think I'll let myself do it." He learned right there that growing up takes time.

Spiritual maturity, like physical maturity, doesn't happen overnight. It takes time. But it also takes determination.

One man challenged me, saying, "Brother, I figure that if God can hear the prayer of a toddler, he can hear me regardless of how I pray."

I assured him that he was correct. "Sure, God can hear you as well as He can hear a toddler. However, is anything more disappointing than a forty-seven-year-old toddler?" Why would anyone settle for such a low goal rather than strive to become the best? Let's discover the elements required to release God's power when we pray. Let's set our sights on becoming those God looks forward to hearing from.

Alice and I once spoke to our children in "baby talk." But as they grew older we changed the way we communicated with them. They are all adults now. Talking in "baby talk" to them would be ridiculous, in spite of the fact that they would understand what we are saying.

It's the same way with prayer. God appreciates the prayer

of toddlers; He loves to hear them pray. Who doesn't? However, there comes a time when we should move from "baby talk" to clear adult communication with God. Prolonged immaturity dishonors Him. What He can hear, or is even willing to hear, isn't the question. The point is *what He deserves to hear,* what brings Him pleasure.

God has delegated dominion of the earth to us and invites us to be His partners in prayer. (See Genesis 1:27–28 and Psalm 115:16.) It's time that we mature in prayer and become intentional, trained allies with God in extending His kingdom on the earth.

Once we become kingdom-oriented, we graduate from problem-centered praying to purpose-driven prayer. We discover that prayer's higher purpose is to accomplish God's eternal agenda. When we begin to "tune our prayers into that frequency," self begins to fade, and Christ becomes the focus of our prayers. Then God will be honored to hear them.

Zachary, one of our grandsons (who was three years old at the time), was spending the night with us. He was having difficulty going to sleep, and because of it, *I* was having difficulty going to sleep! After warning him several times to stop sneaking out of his bed, making noises, and whatever else he could think to do to stay awake, I heard him talking. That was it! I climbed out of bed again, lumbered down the hall to his room, turned on his light, and said sternly, "Zachary Myles Smith, who are you talking to?!"

He sat upright, looked at me with his big brown eyes, and said angelically, "I talkin' to my room."

How about you? Like Zachary, have you felt like you've been talkin' to your room? Have you elevated yourself and your needs above God's agenda? As you grow to maturity, you'll come to understand that prayer is not primarily about you; it's about your heavenly Father and His kingdom.

Prayer's prime purpose has to do with the heart of God. In fact, He promised us that if we'd focus on His kingdom, He'd focus on those things we need. "But seek first his kingdom and his righteousness, and *all these things will be given to you as well*" (Matthew 6:33, emphasis added).

He has called us to a joint venture with Him in the family business, which is building His kingdom! Great communication skills are required to build any effective family business. Prayer is the ultimate wireless communication. May ours always be more than "talkin' to our room."

In the next chapter we will learn about the day prayer changed.

a NEW DAY *brings a* NEW WAY *to* PRAY

(Old Testament vs. New Testament Intercession)

MANY OF THE groceries in our home have expiration dates. In fact, I was taking my vitamins one day and noticed that the label on the bottle read "Expires June 1, 1999." The problem was, it was 2002! Some of us are practicing expired methods of prayer.

When Jesus arrived, He announced a new way of doing things. He did things on the Sabbath that the Pharisees couldn't accept. It was clear that a page of history was turning. Then came the day when, with His disciples, He lifted the Communion cup and said, "This cup is the new covenant in my blood" (Luke 22:20).

The gospels of Matthew, Mark, Luke, and John record a time of transition between the Old and New Testaments. The New Testament doesn't actually begin with Matthew, chapter one. It is a contract, a covenant of blood that began at Calvary.

The New Testament is Jesus' own "last will and testament." Like any person's will, it didn't go into effect until His death. At that point an executor (appointed prior to the individual's death) takes steps to see that the will of the deceased is carried out as written.

Like anyone, Jesus' death activated His will. Remarkably, Jesus rose from the dead three days later to serve as executor of His own will!

When we pray, we are like an attorney that essentially pleads a case before Judge Jehovah in heaven's court. Our requests are based on the contract, the covenant that we have with God. Our contract? It's the New Testament. We are New Testament, not Old Testament, believers. For instance, we don't carry our rebellious teenagers outside the city and stone them to death. Nor do we execute adulteresses when we find them. Why? It's because those were Old Testament requirements. Since we are New Testament Christians, shouldn't we be praying New Testament prayers?

I was about to address several thousand church leaders in a large African prayer and leadership conference. The speaker who preceded me had done something troubling. He'd spent his entire session leading the attendees to pray that God would kill a list of more than twenty Islamic leaders. He called out the name of each leader, and then led the congregation in prayer asking God to kill that individual. Now it was my turn to speak.

I began, "My assigned topic was entitled 'The Principles and Price of Godly Ministry.' My outline is in your handbook. You folks can study my notes on your own time; I'm going to address what just happened here." For the next hour I explained why there are some Old Testament prayers that we shouldn't pray. It's true that David prayed that God would kill his enemies (this is called "imprecatory prayer"), but that's old covenant praying. In the Old Testament, God killed sinners; in the New Testament, He died for them. We're New Testament believers, with a new covenant of mercy!

New covenant believers understand that "the ministry Jesus has received is as superior to [the Old Testament priests] as the covenant of which he is mediator is superior to the old one, and it is founded on better promises" (Hebrews 8:6). This suggests that there are *better ways of praying* available to us than were available to Old Testament believers.

God responds to the prayers of those who love and honor Him. I agree that if we had nothing more than the Old Testament model for prayer, God would hear us. We don't throw out the Old Testament and its prayers. There are many wonderful things we can learn from the Old Testament saints. Theologian Graham Scroggie put it this way: "The New is in the Old contained, and the Old is in the New explained!"[1] Elijah, for example, is commended for the way he prayed. (See James 5:17–18.) We all want to pursue God with the passion of David, a man after God's heart, and with faith like Abraham's.

THE DAY PRAYER CHANGED

At the Passover meal, what we call Communion or the Lord's Supper, Jesus held up the cup and said, "This is my blood of the new testament . . ." (Mark 14:24 KJV). With that act He *announced* the New Testament. Hours later, on the cross of Calvary, Jesus shed His blood and *executed* the New Testament. A testament is a covenant between God and man. With the new covenant in place, prayer changed. There are some stark contrasts between Old Testament and New Testament praying. Let's look, perhaps for the first time, at the unique position the death, burial, resurrection, and ascension of Christ and the advent of His Holy Spirit has given us. Only then will we begin to take full advantage of it and see miraculous things happen in answer to our prayer. Here are a few of those contrasts.

Whose Sacrifice—Ours or His?

Prayer must be offered on the basis of a sacrifice. Consider these Old Testament examples:

- Abraham built an altar and offered a sacrifice of praise after learning that God's promises to him included blessings more numerous than the stars. (See Genesis 15:5–21.)

- Isaac built an altar to the Lord after a visitation from God in the night, telling him not to be afraid, that He would protect and bless him. (See Genesis 26:24–25.)

- Job was diligent about sacrificing too. Each morning he offered sacrifices to God, then prayed for the salvation of his children. (See Job 1:4–5.) *Note:* When God began to restore Job, He instructed Job's friends to "take seven bulls and seven rams and go to my servant Job and sacrifice a burnt offering for yourselves. My servant Job will pray for you, and I will accept his prayer and not deal with you according to your folly. You have not spoken of me what is right, as my servant Job has" (Job 42:8). Wow! Did you notice God's promise regarding Job's prayers? God said, *"I will accept his prayer."* God would give him whatever he asked. What an incredible line of prayer credit!

- Elijah built an altar to God, perhaps the best-known of these images, when he challenged the prophets of Baal. You'll recall that after the prophets of Baal failed to arouse their god, Jehovah sent fire from heaven that consumed Elijah's offering. (See 1 Kings 18.)

In the blazing June Calcutta sun, my son Robert and I stood at the altar within the Temple of Kali, a Hindu goddess. One by one, the temple priests would lead baby goats to the altar, bathe them with soapy water, paint their tiny horns in bright colors, then swiftly behead them with a sharp sword.

As their tiny heads rolled to one side and their blood gushed onto the cobblestone floor, the priest would dip his fingers in their blood and smear it on the foreheads of the Kali worshipers who knelt before him. Frankly, it was a ghastly sight! Then God and I had one of our silent conversations.

I asked, "Father, why do they slaughter these cute little goats?"

He said, "Bloody animal sacrifices were originally my idea."

Moses wrote, "Slaughter the ram. Take some of its blood and rub it on Aaron's right earlobe and on the right earlobes of his sons, on the thumbs of their right hands and on the big toes of their right feet. Sprinkle the rest of the blood against all sides of the Altar" (Exodus 29:20 THE MESSAGE). This passage from the Old Testament sounded a lot like what we were seeing done at the Temple of Kali.

"Oh yeah, I forgot," I said. "But we don't do that anymore. Even the Jews have stopped offering bloody animal sacrifices. So why do they still do it here, today, in the Temple of Kali?"

The Father explained, "Satan makes them do it. He wants to be *like me*. In his rebellion, Satan vowed in Isaiah 14:14 that he would 'be like the Most High' [KJV]. He has imitated me for millennia."

Sure enough, to this day in the city of Calcutta, Satan continues to provoke Kali's worshipers to try to duplicate what God ordered done at the tabernacle in the past.

I pressed further. "But Father, if you no longer demand animal sacrifices, why does Satan *still* make them kill these baby goats? Why is he still stuck in an Old Testament rut?"

God said, "Because *Satan has no son!*"

Satan, who said, "I will be like the Most High," failed to realize that, unlike God, he was not omniscient, omnipresent, and omnipotent, nor did he have a son. In time he would learn that he'd bitten off more than he could chew!

Two thousand years ago, God offered His Son as our sacrificial lamb. In His final moment of agony, Christ announced, "It is finished." Suddenly Satan was dumbstruck. There was nothing he could say or do to match the Father's offer. It was as if the Father's voice echoed through the halls of eternity the word that proclaims victory in a game of chess: "Checkmate! Game over!"

Rejoice, Christian! The bleating of every baby goat that dies today in heathen temples around the world announces a fresh proclamation of this truth: "Satan is a loser. He can never be like the Most High, for Satan has no son!"

New Testament intercessors don't build altars or offer bloody sacrifices as they pray. Our prayers are based on the death of God's sacrificial lamb. Christ became both the altar and the sacrifice upon the altar! (See Hebrews 10:19–22.) Because of this, we can "draw near to God with a sincere heart in full assurance of faith" (Hebrews 10:22).

Worthy or Unworthy to Draw Near to God?

Old Testament saints never prayed with a true sense of worthiness. That's why they approached God by offering a sacrifice and addressed Him as "their God," or as "the God of their fathers." It would never have occurred to them to call Him "Our Father, who art in heaven," or "Abba" (Daddy), as Jesus would later teach us to do. When Elijah prayed, he addressed the "LORD God of Abraham, Isaac, and Israel," and referred to himself as "Your servant" (1 Kings 18:36 NKJV).

In contrast, New Testament intercessors pray *in the name of Jesus* and approach Father God as those *made worthy* by the blood of Christ. We approach God's throne of grace "with confidence, so that we may receive mercy and find grace to help us in our time of need" (Hebrews 4:16).

Follow the transition of intimacy that results from our New Testament status:

- Christ tells us in John 15:15 that we are no longer His servants. We're His *friends*.

- He teaches us that we are *God's children* and should

approach Him as "our Father." (See Matthew 6:9; Romans 8:14–16.)

- In Romans 8:17 we learn that we are *joint heirs with Christ* (NKJV). Isn't that enough? No. There's more. We're more than sons and daughters of God and joint heirs with Christ.

- We are "*Christ's bride*" (see Revelation 22:17). Could anything be more intimate than being His bride, of one spirit with Him? Yes, in fact, there is.

- He tells us we are *members of His body*! (See 1 Corinthians 12:27; Ephesians 5:30.) No one in the Old Testament ever had a clue about any of this. We are incredibly blessed!

Our Power of Attorney

Jesus has given us a tool that the Old Testament saints never had. We have been given His name to use in prayer: "Until now you have asked nothing in My name" (John 16:24 NKJV). No one before He came had ever prayed with this authority—in the name of God's own Son.

Do We Pray According to His Promises or His Provision?

Do you have a storeroom where you keep things you think you *might* need? Some of us have a habit of collecting useless things with the idea that they may come in handy some day. That's me. I have nuts and bolts of a million varieties. *One day,*

I think to myself, *I'll need one of these.* I've had some of them for more than twenty years!

Storerooms can be filled with either useless junk or things that we will truly need in the future. God has a storeroom in heaven with your name on it. Your storeroom contains Calvary's provision, which are His "exceedingly great and precious promises" and "all things that pertain to life and godliness" (2 Peter 1:3–4 NKJV). When Christ said at Calvary, "It is finished," it was! He finished all that His Father had sent Him to do, and now He sits at His Father's right hand.

In the Old Testament, people prayed largely according to God's promises, looking forward to what He would do. We, on the other hand, pray primarily according to Calvary's provision—looking back to what He has done.

It's as if Old Testament saints were saved "on credit," awaiting God's payment for their sin. Every sacrificial lamb that was slain was like the metaphorical swipe of a spiritual credit card. It was an obedient expression of their faith, but it didn't "take away" their sins. The writer of Hebrews explains, "It is impossible for the blood of bulls and goats to take away sins" (Hebrews 10:4).

When Old Testament believers put their trust in God, He *covered* their sin. In Psalm 32:1, David wrote, "Blessed is he whose transgression is forgiven, whose sin is covered" (NKJV). Also see Psalm 85:2–3.

Finally, on Calvary's cross, Jesus paid off their account balance—and ours! "He did not enter by means of the blood of goats and calves; but he entered the Most Holy Place once for all by His own blood, having obtained eternal redemption" (Hebrews 9:12). He no longer covers our sins. Since Calvary, when we confess our sins He forgives us and *cleanses* us from all sin! (See 1 John 1:9 NKJV.)

Today when we pray, we access by faith what has already been given to us; we do not beg God for what we've not yet been given.

Delivered *From* Our Circumstances, or Developed *by* Our Circumstances?

A large portion of our conversations with God stems from our desire to be delivered from our circumstances. In that regard, we're not much different from the Old Testament saints, but shouldn't we be?

- Jacob prayed to be delivered from Esau (Genesis 32:11).

- Moses offered God excuses in response to God's call for him to deliver the Israelites (Exodus 3:12–13).

- Joshua prayed for deliverance after his defeat at Ai (Joshua 7:10–11).

- Naomi prayed for deliverance from her circumstances when, in her grief, she said, "The hand of the Lord has gone out against me" (Ruth 1:13 NKJV).

- Hannah prayed for deliverance from childlessness, fretting that God would never give her a child (1 Samuel 1:10–11).

- David continually prayed for deliverance from his enemies (e.g., Psalm 35).

- King Saul prayed to be delivered from losing his kingdom because of his sin, but he eventually sought counsel from the witch of Endor (1 Samuel 28:5–10).

In the New Testament, we discover a new, higher value. While we can still pray for deliverance (see Matthew 6:13; 2 Corinthians 1:10; Philippians 1:19; 2 Thessalonians 3:2; and 2 Timothy 4:17), deliverance from our circumstances *is not* to be our highest priority. Development *in* our circumstances is. After all, it's ultimately about God's glory, not our comfort. As we go through difficult times we can be comforted by the following truths from Scripture.

- Satan didn't have carte blanche with Job. He couldn't do as he pleased. That's true for us too. When we are living in fellowship with Christ, whatever touches us must first have God's permission.

- God carefully measures our trials, and He promises that we won't face more than we can bear (1 Corinthians 10:13). (But we must also keep in mind that when we choose to walk in darkness, we move out from under God's protection.)

- Trouble is our friend, spiritually speaking. Trouble increases our faith, James says. It forces us to trust God and nothing else. It toughens and strengthens us. It promotes spiritual maturity. It's a witness to others of Christ's sufficiency in our lives.

- There are times when we *should* pray for deliverance from trouble; in the Lord's Prayer Jesus taught us to pray, "Lead us not into temptation, but deliver us from the evil one" (Matthew 6:13). In the garden of Gethsemane Jesus prayed that He would be delivered from the agony of the cross. But in the end, He elevated His Father's will above His own. Our prayer priority should always be for God to be glorified and for His purposes to be fulfilled in our circumstances.

Do you recall when Jesus told Peter, "Satan has asked to sift you as wheat. But I've prayed for you" (Luke 22:31)? Perhaps Peter said to himself, "Whew! Thank God you've prayed for me. I don't think I could stand a satanic sifting right now."

But Jesus hadn't prayed that God would *deliver Peter from* his circumstances. Jesus had prayed that Peter would be *developed by* them. He didn't pray for Peter to be *exempted* from trial. He prayed that Peter would be *increased* by it! It's not what we experience that matters; it's what our experiences produce that matters. Jesus prayed three specific things for Peter:

1. That Peter's faith wouldn't fail.
2. That he would be converted (changed).
3. That the experience would equip him to strengthen others.

As a result, to this very day Peter's experience and the letters he wrote inspire us all.

Can you see the difference in purpose? Old Testament believers tended to focus on deliverance from their circumstances. Because of that, they often prayed anxiety-ridden prayers. King David, who said, "Do not fret because of evil men," and declared, "My soul finds rest in God alone; I will never be shaken" (Psalm 37:1; 62:1–2), also said, "Listen to my prayer, O God, do not ignore my plea. . . . My thoughts trouble me and I am distraught. . . . My heart is in anguish within me; the terrors of death assail me. Fear and trembling have beset me; I cry out in distress" (Psalm 55:1–2, 4–5, 17).

But don't be too critical of David and the other Old Testament believers. They operated according to the revelation they had, and that is how God judges us—according to what we have, not according to what we don't have. (See 2 Corinthians 8:12.) We have more revelation than David had, so God's expectations for us are higher.

We are told in Philippians 4:6: "Do not be anxious about anything, but in everything, by prayer and petition, with thanksgiving, present your requests to God." Rather than try to avoid difficulties, we're told to consider them as opportunities to develop godly character. (See James 1:2–4.) Our priority in prayer should be for God's purposes to be fulfilled, no matter what our circumstances may be. Paul said, "I have learned to be content whatever the circumstances" (Philippians 4:11), and "Godliness with contentment is great gain" (1 Timothy 6:6).

Listen to how Jesus prayed as He thought about His upcoming trial: "Now my heart is troubled, and what shall I say? 'Father, save me from this hour'? No, it was for this very reason [purpose] I came to this hour. Father, glorify your name!" (John 12:27–28). To Jesus there was a higher priority than being exempted from trial. It was for His Father to be glorified in it.

His followers, New Testament Christians, prayed that they would be considered worthy to suffer for Christ's sake! Consider Paul and Silas, who preferred God's purpose to their pleasure:

After they had been severely flogged, they were thrown into prison, and the jailer was commanded to guard them carefully. Upon receiving such orders, he put them in the inner cell and fastened their feet in the stocks. About midnight Paul and Silas were praying and singing hymns to God, and the other prisoners were listening to them. Suddenly there was such a violent earthquake that the foundations of the prison were shaken. At once all the prison doors flew open, and everybody's chains came loose.
ACTS 16:23–26

We all want to have an experience like Paul had. It is interesting to note, however, that Paul, who experienced this earthquake and jailbreak, spent almost the rest of his natural life in prison for Christ's sake.

These people understood . . . "Now if we are children, then we are heirs—heirs of God and co-heirs with Christ, if indeed we share in his sufferings in order that we may also share in his glory" (Romans 8:17). We don't know the prayers the church prayed for Peter when he was in prison. (See Acts 12.) Rather than praying for his release, they were more than likely praying for his strength to withstand the test and for the purposes of God to be fulfilled in his trial. Why do I think this? First, because, as Christ had prayed, Peter had been strengthened during Satan's sifting; this included his denial of Christ at the crucifixion. From that point on, escaping trial wasn't Peter's personal "modus operandi." Another reason is because when Peter appeared at the house where the prayer meeting was going on for him, the person who answered the door couldn't believe it was him. Likely, they never considered that God would answer their prayer in this way!

In Acts 4, Peter and John were arrested for preaching the gospel. "When they" (the Sanhedrin—Jewish judges who oversaw religious rules) "saw the courage of Peter and John and realized that they were unschooled, ordinary men, they were astonished and they took note that these men *had been with Jesus*" (v. 13, emphasis added). After conferring together privately, the Sanhedrin commanded Peter and John not to speak or teach in the name of Jesus.

> But Peter and John replied, *"Judge for yourselves whether it is right in God's sight to obey you rather than God. For we cannot help speaking about what we have seen and heard."*
> ACTS 4:19–20

> Sometimes our circumstances will be difficult because we've chosen to follow Jesus. This is something that we learn to accept. After all, Jesus said, *"If the world hates you, keep in mind that it hated me first."*
> JOHN 15:18

> James, the brother of Jesus, writes, *"My brethren, count it all joy when you fall into various trials, knowing that the testing of your faith produces patience. But let patience have its perfect work, that you may be perfect and complete, lacking nothing."*
> JAMES 1:2–4 NKJV

The New Testament Christian isn't surprised by trouble or put off by it. His only concerns are that it finishes its work in him, that Christ is glorified in it, and that it extends Christ's kingdom.

CURSING VS. BLESSING

It's been said that Old Testament prayers, with the exception of David's, tended to be more "earthly" in their concerns. New Testament prayers tended to be more "heavenly."

When Samson was dying, he asked if he could take vengeance against those who had blinded him. It says in Judges 16:28, "Then Samson prayed to the Lord, 'O Sovereign Lord, remember me. O God, please strengthen me just once more, and let me with one blow get revenge on the Philistines for my two eyes.'"

Contrast Samson's dying prayer to that of Stephen in the New Testament: "While they were stoning him, Stephen prayed, 'Lord Jesus, receive my spirit.' Then he fell on his knees and cried out, 'Lord, do not hold this sin against them.' When he had said this, he fell asleep" (Acts 7:59–60). The New Testament even gives us a new redemptive way to pray for our enemies!

Consider David, who often prayed curses against his physical enemies—both men and nations. Here are some of his prayers gleaned from the Psalms:

- "Shatter the teeth of the enemy."

- "Confuse their counsel."

- "Rebuke them in your anger and terrify them in your wrath."

- "May they fall into the pits that they have dug."

- "May they become ensnared in their own nets."

But in the New Testament, Jesus offers a new perspective: "You have heard that it was said, 'Love your neighbor and hate your enemy.' But I tell you: Love your enemies and pray for those who persecute you, that you may be sons of your Father in heaven" (Matthew 5:43–45).

Jesus' teaching was strange to be sure. He was no ordinary teacher. He was the Prince of Peace, who had come to set things straight, announce a new day, and with it, new ways of relating to God and to men. Gone were the days of vindictive hatred and vengeance. By His sacrifice, Jesus forever calmed God's outraged holiness against our sin. He applied His blood to heaven's mercy seat, and God's mercy has been applied to us. In turn, we are to appeal for mercy on behalf of others. "Mercy triumphs over judgment!" (James 2:13).

> A mother sought the pardon of her son from Napoleon. The emperor said it was his second offense, and justice demanded his death.
>
> "I don't ask for justice," said the mother, "I plead for mercy."
>
> "But," said the emperor, "he does not deserve mercy."
>
> "Sir," cried the mother, "it would not be mercy if he deserved it, and mercy is all I ask for."
>
> "Well then," said Napoleon, "I will have mercy." And her son was saved.[2]

Like Napoleon's problem with this offender, there were certainly many things happening in Israel that could provoke Jesus to desire vengeance. After all, Israel was suffering under ruthless Roman rule. But Jesus never prayed against His enemies, nor did He ever encourage anyone else to do so.

In Luke 9:52–56, we find two of Jesus' disciples, James and John, infuriated over the way a Samaritan village was refusing them passage through their territory. (Perhaps this was a case of first-century road rage.) Dubbed the "Sons of Thunder," in Mark 3:17, they were suffering from OTPS (Old Testament Prophet Syndrome). Remembering how Elijah had called down fire from heaven and ordered the killing of 850 prophets of Baal, they said, "Jesus, what do you say we call down a bolt of lightning and barbeque the whole bunch?"

(my paraphrase). Jesus rebuked them and said, "Guys, that idea didn't originate in heaven. I haven't come here to incinerate folks, but to save them" (my paraphrase, again).

Even dying, when Roman soldiers were executing Jesus, He pled in their defense, saying, "Father, forgive them, for they do not know what they are doing" (Luke 23:34). And with that the Innocent (Christ) became guilty, so the guilty (we) could go free!

Reversing the Cursing?

I met a pastor in a northern state who learned that a local college professor, who was teaching a class on the occult, was cursing him. The pastor retaliated by preaching a message against the occult and in it mentioned the professor and his class. The pastor then led his people to pray that God would multiply the professor's curses and return them to him sevenfold. I'm amazed at how many Christians pray, as they call it, to "reverse the curses" spoken against them.

A number of years ago, on the day before Halloween, dozens of churches in the Houston area hosted a large gathering to worship, to repent for the sins of the city, to be reconciled with each other, and to make a proclamation against darkness. We called it "Breakthrough Houston."

I was leading worship that night and was busy with the last-minute pre-service details as thousands of excited and energetic Christians flooded into the auditorium. Dozens of cooperating pastors were meeting and greeting each other onstage.

In the space of a few minutes, three unrelated individuals spoke to me or handed me notes suggesting that there was an infiltration of witches or Satanists at the event, which had been advertised throughout the city as an alternative to Halloween. One said, "Pastor Eddie, I believe the Lord has told me that there is a group of witches here tonight. What should we do?" My natural inclination might have been to pray for God's hedge of protection around us, or to attempt to bind spirits of darkness. Instead, the Spirit of God led me to do something different.

After the opening praise song and welcome, I took the microphone and said, "Before you are seated, I'm told that there are witches or Satanists with us tonight. If that describes you, we want to take a moment now and welcome you to this event. Be assured that you are surrounded by people who care for you and want nothing less than God's best for you. In fact, you are in the safest place in town. And I want to take a moment to pray for God to bless you." With that, I prayed a sincere prayer for Christ to bless them. Then we continued the program. The night was an awesome success.

At the conclusion of the service, one lady told me, "There was a rather strange-looking woman sitting beside me in the balcony. She didn't stand to sing the first praise song with us. Instead, she sat with her head bowed as if she were praying. On her lap she had arranged a large bronze cross, some other religious-looking icons, and what appeared to be small fetishes. When you welcomed the witches, blessed them, and prayed for them, she grabbed up her paraphernalia and threw it into her large purse and never pulled it out again."

Several participating pastors approached me about this at the conclusion of the service. They all shared the sentiments of one who said, "Wow! What an unusual way to start a service, and what a unique way to deal with such a serious problem. I don't think I would have thought to do what you did. Thank you. That taught me a lot tonight."

I suppose it was an odd approach. In the Old Testament (Exodus 22:18 KJV) they were told not to "suffer a witch to live." God instructed them to kill witches. Personally, I'm grateful to be under the new covenant, because I've led some witches and warlocks to Christ. Today their lives are impacting many others for Jesus.

It's not likely you've focused prayer on the destruction of those who've offended you. But are you asking God to *bless them*? "Do not repay evil with evil or insult with insult, but with blessing, because to this you were called so that you may inherit a blessing" (1 Peter 3:9). And are you loving your enemies?

ENDUED OR INDWELT?
IS THE HOLY SPIRIT ON US, OR IN US?

Only a little over a century ago, vehicles of personal conveyance were horse-drawn. When the combustible engine was placed inside vehicles, the world of transportation was changed forever. To this day, a car's performance is measured in "horse power," but of course the difference between the performance of an automobile and a horse-drawn carriage is enormous. The same can be said for the role of the Holy Spirit in believers' lives from the old to the new covenant. In the Old Testament, the Holy Spirit occasionally *came upon* people and endued, or clothed, them with power. He was external to them. But on the Day of Pentecost, when the Holy Spirit came to empower men *from the inside,* everything changed!

In the Old Testament, Samson was endued with the Holy Spirit's power many times. But there came a day when, because of his sin, God's Spirit left him powerless. "Then she [Delilah] called, 'Samson, the Philistines are upon you!' He awoke from his sleep and thought, 'I'll go out as before and shake myself free.' But he did not know that the Lord had left him" (Judges 16:20).

Unlike in Samson's day, today if we belong to God, the Holy Spirit *constantly lives in us*. He is an internal source of power in our lives. "You, however, are controlled not by the sinful nature but by the Spirit, if the Spirit of God lives in you. And if anyone does not have the Spirit of Christ, he does not belong to Christ" (Romans 8:9).

PRAYING FOR OURSELVES VS. PRAYING FOR OTHERS

In the Old Testament, we see intercessors praying on behalf of others. The prophets often bore the burden of the entire nation in their prayers. However, there is still a significant difference in the majority of prayers recorded in the Old Testament compared to those recorded in the New Testament. If we just look at David compared to Paul, for instance, we see that David tended to focus on his own concerns, while Paul prayed day and night for other believers. Here is an example of what Paul prayed:

> *For this reason, since the day we heard about you, we have not stopped praying for you and asking God to* fill you with the knowledge of his will through all spiritual wisdom and understanding. *And we pray this in order that* you may live a life worthy of the Lord *and*

may please him in every way: bearing fruit in every good work, growing in the knowledge of God, being strengthened with all power according to his glorious might *so that you may* have great endurance and patience, *and* joyfully giving thanks to the Father, *who has qualified you to share in the inheritance of the saints in the kingdom of light. For he has rescued us from the dominion of darkness and brought us into the kingdom of the Son he loves, in whom we have redemption, the forgiveness of sins.*
COLOSSIANS 1:9–14, EMPHASIS ADDED

Paul's personal prayer requests interest me. Not that you shouldn't, but we never read of Paul requesting prayer for a backache or a head cold. He asked others to pray that he would faithfully preach the gospel. It seems that some Christians today expect to have a trouble-free life. Few of us have seen or experienced true hardship—especially for the gospel's sake!

Although imprisoned and in chains, Paul never prayed for, nor asked anyone else to pray for, his release. Here is a sample of what Paul requested that others would pray for him:

Devote yourselves to prayer, being watchful and thankful. And pray for us, too, that God may open a door for our message, so that we may proclaim the mystery of Christ, for which I am in chains. Pray that I may proclaim it clearly, as I should.
COLOSSIANS 4:2–4

God's Prayer Partners

During his thirty-three years living as a man on this planet, Jesus spent an extraordinary amount of time in prayer. But what does He do now? The writer of Hebrews tells us:

> *Jesus has become the guarantee of a better covenant. Now there have been many of those [Old Testament] priests, since death prevented them from continuing in office; but because Jesus lives forever,* he has a permanent priesthood. *Therefore he is able to save completely those who come to God through him, because* he always lives to intercede for them. *Such a high priest meets our need—one who is holy, blameless, pure, set apart from sinners, exalted above the heavens.*
> HEBREWS 7:22–26, EMPHASIS ADDED

What is the job of a priest? A priest is a go-between, someone who stands between earth and heaven on behalf of others—an advocate, a "spiritual attorney," a mediator, an intercessor. But Jesus is more than a priest, He is "a great high priest"! When we pray, we have the assurance that Jesus prays for us. He's our prayer partner!

But that's not all. God partners in another way with us in prayer. We've all faced circumstances that were too complex or too devastating for us to craft the words to pray. In Romans 8:26–27, we read:

> *In the same way, the Spirit helps us in our weakness. We do not know what we ought to pray for, but the Spirit himself intercedes for us with groans that words cannot express. And he who searches our hearts knows the mind of the Spirit, because the Spirit intercedes for the saints in accordance with God's will.*

We don't just pray *to* God, we pray *with* God. The prayers God answers are those prayed in accordance with His will. The Holy Spirit "searches all things, even the deep things of God," and "knows the thoughts of God." Best of all, He's in us! We have "the mind of Christ." (See 1 Corinthians 2:10–11, 16.)

How great it is to have God himself as our prayer partner! Through the wisdom the Holy Spirit provides, we are able to pray more effectively for the things that matter in His kingdom. He will lead us not only to pray about the right things but also to approach the throne room with the right attitude. We'll look at that next.

THRONE ROOM ETIQUETTE

One minute (David) the young son of Jesse had been a national hero eating royal dainties off platters of beaten gold, a close companion of King Saul, married to the king's daughter, best buds with Prince Jonathan. And then, such a short time later, he found himself crouching in the dark depths of a limestone cave, hiding from Saul's death squads. He was on the run—a wanted man and a fugitive—for the next 15 years.

Hungry, thirsty, cold, and gripped with fear, David pleaded, "Listen to my cry, for I am in desperate need" (Psalm 142:6). Or as *The Message* renders it, "Oh listen, please listen; I've never been this low."

David yelled his fears. He made demands. He warned God to act quickly, because he was walking on the ragged edge of sanity, and the dirt under his feet was beginning to crumble.

Most likely in those same terrible days, he scratched graffiti like this on the walls of his cave: *"You'd better listen to me and listen to me now. I'm like a match flame in a gust of wind, and if You don't do something fast I'm done. Get with it, God. Help. Come. Don't step away from me now. I'm on the edge and I'm losing my balance."*[3]

I once had a prayer partner who, when we prayed, would pace back and forth, shaking his fist in the air, passionately making demands of God. He'd yell things like: "God, I'm tired of crying out to you about this. It's time for you to move and move *now*. I expect you to settle this issue, God."

One day I thought, *My goodness. I wouldn't dare speak to my earthly father with such a demanding tone. I would never "order" my father to do anything, let alone my heavenly Father.* Before I proceed, however, let me make one thing clear. My friend was praying at the level of his revelation. That's all any of us can do. The main thing was that he was praying. Our merciful Father heard and answered his prayer in spite of what I saw as a less-than-respectful way of addressing Him. At the same time, Scripture does show us things that will help us to approach God in ways that will enhance our prayer partnership with Him.

Our Advantages

Today, you and I have many advantages that biblical characters never had. That's the good news. The bad news is that we will be held accountable for them. Let me point out a few:

- We relate to God under a new covenant—a revised contract. We have the Holy Spirit in us. We have been given more revelation than anyone who is mentioned in Scripture (Old or New Testaments). We live on "the power side" of the cross. The blood has been shed, applied to the mercy seat, and Christ has conquered sin, hell, and the grave. It is finished! As stated earlier, we've been given "exceedingly great and precious promises" and "everything that pertains to life and godliness."

- We have the complete canon of Scripture.

- We have two thousand years of church history behind us.

The day and time in which we live was a mystery, hidden from Old Testament saints. They knew where they were and the bondage under which they suffered. They also knew about a coming King who would one day set up His kingdom and rule the earth. But they had no understanding of the two thousand years between, what we call the "church age." They had none of the lessons we've learned from them.

One night in a prayer meeting, one of our ladies prayed, "O Lord, rend the heavens and come down," from Isaiah 64:1. Later I told her with a smile, "Mary, you're two thousand years too late. He's already done that! Now He wants to 'rend us' and come out!"

Are you beginning to get the picture? Shouldn't we pray more mature prayers than those prayed in the Old Testament? We have a fuller revelation and enjoy a special relationship with Jehovah that Old Testament believers never dared to imagine. For that reason, we should pray with greater love, gratitude, faith, and fervor than our Old Testament brothers and sisters. Our prayer lives should be more mature than theirs because . . . "From everyone who has been given much, much will be demanded; and from the one who has been entrusted with much, much more will be asked" (Luke 12:48).

the POWER
of PRAYER

ONE DAY I received a call from a New York magazine editor who was writing a story about the prayer movement in America. "Is this Reverend Smith?" she asked.

I said, "No ma'am."

She said, "I'm sorry, I asked to speak to Eddie Smith."

"That's me," I replied.

"Oh good, this *is* Reverend Smith," she said with a bit of relief.

"No ma'am," I explained. "I am not a reverend."

"I'm sorry," she apologized. "I was told that you are a minister."

"I am a minister," I acknowledged.

Puzzled, she asked, "You are a minister, but you're not a reverend—is that even possible?"

I assured her that it was.

She followed with, "And what religion are you?"

"I don't have a religion," I answered.

Somewhat shocked, she said, "You're *a reverend* without *a religion?*"

"No ma'am," I explained dryly, "I'm *not* a reverend . . . *without* a religion."

"Why don't you have a religion?" she pressed.

"Because God hates them," I said.

"I thought religion was God's idea," she said with bewilderment.

"No ma'am," I leveled. "God's idea is *relationship.*"

There was a long, pregnant pause, after which she said with an emotional crack in her voice, "Eddie? I wish you had a church in New York City. I think I would like to attend it."

God has created you for ministry. But true spiritual ministry is based on relationship. Don't confuse it with a public, professional occupation. The saints (all believers) are to be equipped and released in the work of the ministry. Professional clergy isn't by any stretch the pinnacle profession, any more than an NFL coach can be the MVP (Most Valuable Player) of a Super Bowl game. Rightly functioning clergy are coaches. Believers are the players who should be equipped to do true spiritual ministry (the works of the Father in the power of the Spirit) as Christ did!

Our extraordinary God does the extraordinary. He created the earth, sent the flood, split the sea, and performed so many other amazing things. But I'm not referring to what He did but to what He *does*. I'm afraid many of us have allowed an unbiblical disconnect between *what He once did* and *what He does now*. We've arbitrarily determined that although He once did the *extraordinary*, today He only does the more *ordinary*.

Perhaps that's because we see so little of the extraordinary in our lives.

God has told us to call on Him and He will show us *great and mighty things*. He describes the things He will do as "fenced in and hidden, [things] which you do not know (do not distinguish and recognize, have knowledge of and understand)" (Jeremiah 33:3 AMP).

In the New Testament, God presents himself as one "Who, by (in consequence of) the [action of His] power that is at work within us, is able to [carry out His purpose and] do superabundantly, far over and above all that we [dare] ask or think—infinitely beyond our highest prayers, desires, thoughts, hopes or dreams—To Him be glory" (Ephesians 3:20–21 AMP). His "great and mighty things" are beyond our imagination.

Miracles are God's "business cards." They should be routinely evident in our lives. In Acts 19:11, we read that the Lord did special miracles. It appears that normal, everyday miracles weren't enough; God did "extraordinary miracles through Paul."

Powerful demonstrations of His power announce where God is. If we don't see the work of God in our lives, either we aren't in step with Him or we aren't noticing what He is doing. Make no mistake, life can certainly be mundane. But even in our day-to-day lives, miracles can and should occur. Where God is, His signs and wonders are always evident. Paul said, "My message and my preaching were not with wise and persuasive words, but with a demonstration of the Spirit's power" (1 Corinthians 2:4). Paul described the demonstrations of the Spirit in his life this way. He said, "No eye has seen, no ear has heard, no mind has conceived what God has prepared for those who love him" (1 Corinthians 2:9). These passages indicate the Father's intention toward us and His power available to us!

J. Hudson Taylor, beloved missionary to China, said,

> Prayer power has never been tried to its full capacity in any church. If we want to see mighty wonders of divine power and grace wrought in the place of weakness, failure, and disappointment, let the whole church answer God's standing challenge, "Call unto me, and I will answer thee, and show thee great and mighty things, which thou knowest not!"[1]

While I was in Nigeria to speak at a huge prayer and leadership conference, I felt the Lord tell me, at the end of one of the sessions, to ask one of the other speakers if he would pray for me. So I slipped over to him privately and asked if he would. He graciously agreed and suggested that I come to his hotel room on Saturday morning following the conference.

Saturday I awoke, dressed, and called a cab. When I arrived at the hotel where my friend was staying, it appeared as though some sort of business meeting, wedding, or family reunion was about to begin. Entire families were filling the foyer of the hotel and the registration area. I asked the clerk for what occasion they were gathered. He explained, "They hope to get an audience with the evangelist." I was impressed and a little distressed. I said, "I think I have an appointment with him." The clerk looked at the list and said, "Yes, sir. You should go up to his room now."

When I entered his room, which was Spartan by Western standards, I sat down with him and we chatted for a moment. Then my Nigerian friend began to pray. The Lord began to speak hidden things to him about me and my family, none of which he could naturally know. Today, I can report to you that almost every one of his words has come to pass. His prayer was powerfully anointed. That day I experienced a miracle.

Jesus never had trouble drawing a crowd. His problem was escaping the crowds! Why? Everywhere He went, people saw demonstrations of the Spirit's power—the same power that's available to us today.

Pastor and author Chuck Swindoll has said, "Heaven is filled with a room that will surprise all of us when we see it. The room has within it large boxes neatly packaged with a lovely ribbon on top with your name on it. 'Never delivered to Earth because never requested from Earth.' "[2]

WHY GOD WORKS MIRACLES

We live in a day and hour when the Father looks for ways to "show His power off." Here are several reasons why that is.

- *God does the miraculous to indicate His presence.* He told Moses that He would harden Pharaoh's heart "so that my wonders may be multiplied in Egypt" (Exodus 11:9).

- *God does miracles to announce His Son.* Some miracles are signs to make people wonder. They are "brilliant, flashing neon lights" that point people to Jesus Christ, the Savior. After all, it does little good to be healed of cancer, die years later, and spend eternity in hell. Miracles are often a way to introduce people to the risen Savior. (See Mark 16:17–18.)

- *God does miracles to announce His sons.* Jesus promised us that the things He did, we would do, and even greater things. I talk about the "greater things" in our book *Intercessors and Pastors: The Emerging Partnership of Watchmen and Gatekeepers.* Here's a "teaser": The works He promised that we would do are greater in "quality," not in "quantity." Hmmm . . .

- *God performs miracles to be acknowledged.* If you read through the Bible you will be amazed at how important it is to God that He be recognized and remembered for what He does. It's a big deal to Him! He established the feasts in order that man might remember Him. (See Exodus 12 and Deuteronomy 16.)

- *God demonstrates His power to accomplish His purposes.* "Now this is the confidence that we have in Him, that if we ask anything according to His will [His purpose], He hears us. And if we know that He hears us, whatever we ask, we know that we have the petitions that we have asked of Him" (1 John 5:14–15 NKJV). Catherine Marshall said, "The purpose of all prayer is to find God's will and to make that will our prayer."[3]

- *God works miraculously to keep His promises to us.* "Scripture records 7,959 promises God has given to us. If we 'cashed' one each day, it would take us 22 years to use each promise one time. Caleb lived on one promise for 40 years! How many years can we live on 7,959 promises?"[4]

Prayer isn't to *change* God's purpose—it's to *discover* it. We begin with His promises as revealed in His Word. To know

God's promises, learn His Word. God's purposes are like gold waiting to be mined from His promises.

His promises are molds into which we pour our prayers. Our prayers are the molds into which God pours His provision.

Praying His Promises

So if we know His promises, we know how we should pray. Here are a few of His promises. As you read them, ask yourself what they tell you about God's purposes.

- Romans 8:1 says: "Therefore, there is now no condemnation for those who are in Christ Jesus." We're free from condemnation because the Spirit of life has set us free. What a wonderful promise!

- Galatians 4:4–7 says: "But when the time had fully come, God sent his Son, born of a woman, born under law, to redeem those under law, that we might receive the full rights of sons. Because you are sons, God sent the Spirit of his Son into our hearts, the Spirit who calls out, '*Abba,* Father.' So you are no longer a slave, but a son; and since you are a son, God has made you also an heir." We're adopted into God's family in accordance with the Lord's pleasure and His perfect will. This truth liberates us to pray for others to know this glorious relationship with God.

- Philippians 4:13 says: "I can do everything through him who gives me strength." There's nothing in this life we can't conquer because Jesus Christ gives us the strength to love and serve Him.

It's amazing how encouraging just three of His promises can be! Through prayer the Ruler of the Universe invites us to fellowship with Him! And not "by appointment only," as was the case in the Old Testament when the high priest (always a man, never a woman), one time each year, could enter His presence, within the Holy of Holies in the earthly tabernacle. But now any of us can enter the Holy of Holies in the heavenly tabernacle, anytime, and experience immediate, intimate fellowship with Almighty God.

The Old Testament high priest would do so tentatively, with a rope tied around his ankle so he could be extracted (dragged out) if he displeased God and God killed him. Not so with us. We are permitted to enter boldly! (See Hebrews 4:16 NKJV.)

Effective prayer may be the final frontier for the church to conquer before we see God's kingdom rule established and the knowledge of His glory cover the earth. (See Psalm 24:1 and Habakkuk 2:14.) Let's not miss our day of visitation. Who knows? Perhaps it can be said of us as was said of Queen Esther, that we have come into the kingdom for such a time as this! (See Esther 4:14.)

BALANCING RESULTS WITH RELATIONSHIP

My friend missionary/author John DeVries, in his wonderful book *Does It Pay to Pray?* addresses the necessary balance between results and relationship. To expect results in prayer, without developing a relationship with God, is ludicrous. To develop a relationship with God, without expecting results, insults God. The very question "Does it pay to pray?" smacks of American entrepreneurialism, doesn't it? It implies, "If it doesn't pay, I won't pray." But the truth is, *it does pay*. God acts in direct response to our prayer. But that's not the only reason we pray.

Prayer is more than talking to, or working with, God. True prayer is *communing* as well as *communicating* with Him. We pray, as DeVries points out, for the sake of our relationship with God. That is equal in importance to obtaining the results we seek. We are to balance the two. Like any other father, your Father God loves to hear the sound of your voice. Alice and I have two daughters. My heart melts when either of them calls and says, "Daddy?" Well, your Daddy God wants to hear from you too.

PRAYER WORKS

The children of Israel had no sooner escaped Egyptian bondage when they were attacked by the fierce Amalekites. So young Joshua pulled together an army to engage them. Moses, who was well beyond the age of battle, stood atop a hill overlooking the battleground where he lifted his staff above his head and prayed. As Moses prayed, Joshua and his army were successful. But the moment Moses' arms came down, the tide of battle turned against them.

Can't you just see them? Moses prays, and Amalekite soldiers fall impaled with spears, shot with arrows, pierced with swords. Moses pauses to rest, to catch his breath, and suddenly Israeli husbands, fathers, and sons fall dead to the ground. What an example of the power of prayer!

Finally, exhausted, Moses sat down on a large stone to pray

while Aaron and Hur held up his hands for him. As Moses prayed with his hands raised to heaven, Joshua's army was victorious. The battle was won in direct correlation to Moses' prayers. Prayer worked! (See Exodus 17:8–13.)

Sickly King Hezekiah lay on his death bed. He cried out to God in prayer. Before the prophet Isaiah could leave his palace, God told Isaiah to tell the king, "I have heard your prayer and seen your tears: I will heal you." God gave the king fifteen more years of life! Again, prayer worked. (See 2 Kings 20:5.)

Several years ago my dear father, Dr. Robert E. Smith, a pastor for almost fifty-six years, lay at death's door in a Tyler, Texas, hospital. The medical team advised the family to make his funeral arrangements. They explained that Dad wouldn't be returning home from the hospital. However, in answer to prayer, God raised him up and gave us four and a half more years with him.

In our book *Intercessors: How to Understand and Unleash Them for God's Glory*, I write:

> One morning my wife, Alice, went shopping for building supplies for a project I was working on. Being an intercessor and not a construction worker, she was largely unfamiliar with these items and spent a considerable amount of time in the hardware store looking for them.
>
> Alice was finally standing in the checkout line, when suddenly, she had a brief vision. In her mind's eye—a closed vision—she saw a man standing in my office pointing a gun at me.
>
> She immediately grabbed her purse, abandoned her cart with the items she had worked so hard to find, and ran to the car. Alice began to intercede, even as she drove home. Once home, she rushed inside to her prayer closet,

where she began crying out to the Lord.

She has since been asked, "Alice, why didn't you call the office and ask if he was all right?"

"It was time to pray, not take a survey," she replies.

Alice prayed for forty-five minutes until the burden and the sense of urgency subsided. Only then did she call the office and ask, "Eddie, are you okay?"

"Yeah, fine," I answered. "Why do you ask?"

She told me about her vision and how she had entered into prayer.

"Oh that," I explained. "He just got saved."

That morning I had had a counseling session with a medical doctor who was in ill health, separated from his wife, addicted to narcotics, and suicidal. After I led him to Christ—and through some significant deliverance—he explained how he had loaded a pistol that morning and placed it on his kitchen counter, intending to bring it to my office and first kill me, then himself. For some "unexpected reason," he absentmindedly left the pistol on the kitchen counter.

Yes, being married to an intercessor definitely has its advantages![5]

I've seen prayer change others. And I've seen prayer change me. I know prayer can change you. Prayer works.

In his *Praying Church Sourcebook*, prayer leader Alvin Vander Griend tells of a church in Phoenix, Arizona, and their experience with answered prayer. The church picked 160 homes from their neighborhood telephone directory. They divided them into two groups. For ninety days they prayed over eighty of the families. The other eighty families weren't prayed for.

At the end of the ninety days they called each of the 160 homes. The callers identified themselves and what church they were from; then they explained that they were not prospecting for the church—they simply wanted to drop by to pray for the family and for any needs that they might have. They explained that they wouldn't ask to come in.

Of the eighty non-prayed-for homes, only one family invited them to come by. Of the eighty homes for which they had prayed for ninety days, sixty-nine families invited them to come by. As they did, forty-five families actually invited the church team inside to pray! Again, prayer works.

Larry Rieck, elder brother of my friend John Rieck of Houston, Texas, was a safety and security officer at Southwest Baptist University in Boliver, Missouri. Because of his love for the students and his deep commitment to Christ, Larry was known to many as the university's "Nighttime Minister."

On November 12, 2003, Larry went to be with the Lord. At Larry's funeral, his friend Zeke Clawson offered a eulogy. He reported, "One night Larry was called over to a dorm where a very upset football player had just kicked in a car door and ripped off the rearview mirror because he was so angry at the owner.

"When Officer Larry walked into the dorm in uniform and found the young man, he told him he would have to ask him some questions. 'But first,' he said, 'let's pray.' Legend has it that, when the prayer was over, the young man was in tears, repenting for all the sin in his life. I heard he confessed to stealing candy at age five. Then he promised to turn himself in and pay for the repairs. When Larry prayed, things happened." That's power in prayer!

Some of us fail to see the value of the *relational* side of prayer, while others fail to see the value of the *results* side of prayer.

To understand, appreciate, and appropriate the *relational*

aspect of prayer, I recommend my wife's classic bestseller *Beyond the Veil: Entering Into Intimacy With God Through Prayer.* To understand, appreciate, and appropriate the *results aspect* of prayer . . . keep reading.

God's Green Card (Work Permit)

I was reared in McAllen, Texas, five miles from the Texas/Mexico border. Millions of Mexican citizens live along the Rio Grande River that separates our countries. We've heard a lot about illegal immigration in recent years. However, every day thousands of Mexican people work at jobs in the United States during the day and return home to Mexico each evening. A "Green Card" (work permit) from the U.S. government is required for them to do so legally.

When we, those to whom God has given dominion over the earth, pray, we offer God a "Green Card" that authorizes Him to work in our lives and in the lives of others for whom we are praying. Why does God wait for our invitation before He moves? Here's an illustration that may help us understand.

The contractor who built our house in northwest Houston had keys to all of the outside doors. He was the one who bought and installed the locks. But once we signed the papers at closing and took possession of the house, he gave us the keys.

Even though he built our house, he wouldn't think of walking, uninvited, through our front door today. In the same way, our heavenly Father often finds himself standing outside, knocking at the door of our lives, waiting for us to open the door and invite Him in. (See Revelation 3:20.) He sees distressing things happening in our lives, in the lives of our loved ones, and in the nations. He's brokenhearted about them, because He alone holds the answers. But in many cases we don't pray and give Him access to those situations.

Turning on the Faucet

Almost every home in McAllen, Texas, was connected to the Rio Grande River through a system of canals when I was a child. Each lawn in a neighborhood had an irrigation valve. On certain days of the week, homeowners were allowed to open the valve and irrigate their yards with four to six inches of life-giving river water. Needless to say, the lawns in McAllen were and still are beautiful. And what a great time we children had playing in a yard filled with water. It was more than a Slip 'n Slide. We felt as if we had our own ocean!

When we pray focused, purposeful prayers, we open the valve that releases heaven's supply to earth's needs. It is the act of praying that allows the life-giving Spirit of God access to the hearts, lives, and circumstances of people for whom we are praying.

The amazing outpourings we've seen in our generation in South Korea, Guatemala, the Fiji Islands, Argentina, Nigeria, Uganda, and other African nations have resulted from fervent prayers due to disaster. Those disasters have been the result of tyrannical rule, war, famine, epidemics, or economic ruin. When God's people come to the end of themselves, they pray fervently, desperately . . . and God graciously answers. As someone has rightly said, "You don't know that God is all you need until God is all you have!"

Christian leaders, knowing this, often urge us to pray desperate prayers. One of my favorite worship choruses says, "I'm desperate for you." We sing it. But are we *desperate* for Him? Do our everyday lives indicate that desperation, or is it just a figure of speech? (Desperation for God is spiritual hunger—a longing for more of Him.)

THE DESPERATION DILEMMA

Like most sincere, committed Christians, I long to see revival and spiritual awakening in America and around the world. I understand that it typically follows desperate praying. But I'm willing to admit I'm not desperate. I have the desire, but not the desperation.

I also know for a fact that I can't *make* myself desperate, any more than I can force myself to like strawberry ice cream. Sure, disaster often brings desperation. Should I then pray for personal or national disaster in order to become desperate? Or should I just fake it? Surely not. I've dubbed this "the desperation dilemma."

Seems to me, the best thing to do with a dilemma is present it to God. So I did. Here is what I think He's shown me. It isn't our desperation that pleases God. In fact, because of His great love for us, He is saddened by our desperation. Our loving Father finds no pleasure in watching us suffer, any more than we would be pleased to see our children suffer. It isn't desperation that He desires. What He longs to see in us is *the fruit of desperation*. But what is that?

The Key: The Fruit of Desperation

Desperation is a tool that readies us, and draws us, to *acknowledge* and *trust* God. This is what brings Him pleasure.

Can we acknowledge and trust Him apart from disaster? Is there a route, short of disaster, that would lead us to that end? I believe there is. I believe there's a glorious route that leads to God's pleasure, His sheer delight—a route that releases His favor. That route is an attitude of *gratitude*.

As I visit developing nations where God is at work, I find Christians who are thankful for even the smallest expression of God's favor. I've become acquainted with a beautiful former pastor's wife, who is "mother" to seventy-four orphaned children in a tin-roofed mud hut in India, and who is utterly grateful. She runs the orphanage because she's widowed. She awoke one morning to find her dear husband's body severed into seven pieces, lying on their front lawn. The couple wouldn't compromise their convictions for Christ, and the pastor paid for it with his life. But this hasn't deterred his wife one bit. She's a vibrant Christian woman with a heart full of gratitude.

I also have a friend in Pakistan who, one Sunday morning in 2002, was sitting in a church in Islamabad when a Muslim extremist tossed a "live" grenade into his lap. In his attempt to save others, his leg was blown off, his stomach was filled with shrapnel, and one of his beautiful daughters was instantly killed. In spite of what he has experienced—disappointment, disability, and intense discomfort at times—he is nevertheless grateful to God.

As my son Robert and I were leaving the Temple of Kali in Calcutta, India, an Indian pastor's nineteen-year-old son asked me to pray for him.

"What do you want me to pray?" I asked.

He said, "Pray that God will find me worthy to suffer for Christ's sake."

I turned to Robert and said, "Many Western Christians

would have said, 'For Christ's sake, why should I suffer?'"
Could it be that the greatest sin in America is our sin of
ingratitude? Let's repent, and begin to pray with thanksgiving,
acknowledging God as we should. And let's raise our focus
from merely our wants and wishes, even our needs, to those
things that are on God's heart. Here's a clue. The Father's
focus today is on His kingdom.

I believe your life will be transformed in the next few
chapters as we begin to put it all together for His glory!

it's about
THE KINGDOM

IN THE 1990s, Alice and I were pastors of an amazing church in Houston, Texas. We had a slogan that I picked up from our friends Ace and Joy Clarke, pastors of the Joshua Center in Hamilton, Ontario, Canada. The slogan was:

> *It's not about you,*
> *It's not about me,*
> *It's about the kingdom.*

Why is that so important? Because in more than forty-five years of ministry, I've noticed that many of the people in the average church think it's about *them*. And others think the pastor thinks it's about *him*. So Alice and I continually reminded ourselves and our members that it was not about us or them; it was about God's kingdom.

Everything is about the kingdom. God has created all things for His pleasure. Our friend Tommy Tenney says, "God has a funny idea. He thinks it's all about Him." It's not merely about building a great church, an effective ministry, or taking a city. It is, and will always be, about Jesus Christ—the King and His kingdom.

One of the fine men in our church, Charles (not his real name), once asked, "Pastor Eddie, if you get a chance next Sunday night, could we sing my favorite song, 'One Day at a Time'?"

"Charles," I replied dryly, "we don't worship you." Odd sense of humor, I know. But there's a significant point there.

A BIGGER VIEW OF FATHER GOD

In 1957, when I was in high school, my father pastored First Baptist Church in McAllen, Texas. I recently found an old 1957 Texas Baptist Annual that listed church statistics of that year. Curious, I looked up First Baptist, McAllen. To my amazement, I discovered that Dad's church averaged over seven hundred people in Sunday school attendance that year, in a town where non-Catholics comprised only 3 percent of the population. That's considered a large church by today's standards. But for that time and place, his was a megachurch! Interestingly, when I was a child, although I knew he was a wonderful dad, it never dawned on me that my father was a particularly *successful* pastor.

Then I thought about our four children. It wasn't until they were adults that they began to grasp that Mom and Dad are *more than* Mom and Dad. They began to understand that we are people with dreams, responsibilities, demanding roles, and levels of influence outside of the family. As children they assumed, as we all did, that Mom and Dad's world revolved primarily around them.

During our first few years of life, we related to our parents according to *who they were to us*. We had tunnel vision. As preschool children, we knew our fathers only in their role as "Daddy." Caring for our needs was their only role in life—wasn't it? We were blissfully unaware that our daddy was an attorney, a doctor, a factory worker, a farmer, a manager, or that he held any other position or had any responsibility other than our care.

In time, our view began to broaden. If you had siblings, you began to realize that your parents were their parents too. Gradually your parents' other roles began to register with you. You discovered that they shared a relationship with each other that hardly included you—they were husband and wife. Who knew?! And, although differently for each of us, we eventually discovered that our parents had relationships, roles, and responsibilities outside the home that were not newly acquired; they'd had these all along. We were simply becoming aware of them.

The same is true with our heavenly Father and our relationship to Him through prayer. Most of us realized the importance of prayer in a time of need. If you've been praying since childhood, you came to God as you were instructed by your parents, teachers, and pastors. You likely learned to pray when you were fearful, or when you wanted something. Prayer was little more than that.

If you came to God for the first time as an adult, perhaps you learned to pray as a result of the death of a loved one, a divorce, or a job loss. Adults typically come to God in prayer because they have a need. It isn't *wrong* to pray in these circumstances; God is here to meet our needs. But that isn't where our prayers should stop. There's much more!

A KING AND HIS KINGDOM

It's time for us to climb to the summit, look over the crest of this mountain, and view the vast horizon. From here, we can see things beyond—the expanse of eternity lies before us. We can get a great view of God's kingdom, our place, and the place of prayer in it.

Jesus rules a spiritual kingdom that will never pass away. The psalmist said, "Your kingdom is an everlasting kingdom, and your dominion endures through all generations" (Psalm 145:13). Jesus began His earthly ministry with an announcement that His kingdom, the kingdom of God, was at hand. Jesus conquered Satan when He defeated death and the grave, ascended into heaven, and sat down at the right hand of the Father. (See Hebrews 1:3–4.) Our greatest enemy isn't Satan. Our greatest enemy is ignorance—ignorance about God's kingdom. What is it that Jesus wants us to know about His dominion?

The word *kingdom* comes from several Greek words that, woven together, provide a powerful definition. My paraphrase would be that "The kingdom is governed by a sovereign royal ruler, a king." Jesus Christ is the rightful ruler of a spiritual kingdom, and one day, all men will bow before Him. (See Philippians 2:9–10.) Scripture teaches that, once we were made the righteousness of God through the work of Jesus Christ, we also became priestly kings, or kingly priests, in Christ's kingdom (2 Corinthians 5:21; Revelation 1:6).

As priests, we are Christ's prayer partners. How's that?

Today He sits at the right hand of the Father, interceding for us. (See Hebrews 7:25.) As kings, *with a small "k,"* we are to exercise our earth-realm dominion that God gave man in the garden of Eden. Jesus Christ is described as the King of Kings (King over us). He is the great King, He is our King, and we are described as lesser kings.

When Queen Victoria of England, who ruled the English monarchy for sixty-four years (the longest reign in that country to date), celebrated the fiftieth anniversary of her coronation, she walked the aisle of Westminster Abbey past the grave of David Livingstone (1813–1873). Livingstone, a Scottish medical missionary, was one of the greatest European explorers of Africa. He helped open the hearts of Africans to the gospel.

Inscribed on Livingstone's gravestone are the words of Christ, taken from John 10:16 (KJV): "Other sheep I have, which are not of this fold." Queen Victoria only ruled for sixty-four years. Our King's rule will never end! It is a kingdom without end. As His administrative, earthly kings and priests, we are charged with the task of "praying in the harvest," praying for the billions of "sheep" (lost men, women, boys, and girls) who are not yet in the fold.

Jesus pointed out that, once we are born again, the kingdom of God is *inside us!* (See Luke 17:21.) It's the mysterious doctrine of interpenetration: Christ and His kingdom are *in us* and we are *in Christ and His kingdom.* Paul described this mystery when he said, "And God raised us up with Christ and seated us with him in the heavenly realms in Christ Jesus" (Ephesians 2:6). Our primary job on earth, then, is to seek first His kingdom in everything. When we do, He promises us clearly that everything else will fall into place.

We are living in the day of rediscovering God's purposes

for us within His kingdom. As we put His kingdom first, God's purposes for us become clearer. Here are a few of those purposes:

- *Dominion.* God has given us dominion (rulership) of the earth (Genesis 1:26; Psalm 115:16). With the spiritual authority given to us as ambassadors of God's kingdom, we are to proclaim the good news of His kingdom throughout the earth. Jesus told us that we would preach this gospel throughout the earth right before His second coming. (See Matthew 24:14.)

  One of the Greek words for *kingdom* is *baino,* which means to walk, or to pace off the land with the foot. As official representatives of the kingdom of heaven, we are to be pacing the land with the message of Christ and seeking first His kingdom as we declare His message, which is "Repent, for the kingdom of heaven is at hand" (Matthew 4:17 NKJV).

- *Administration.* Before leaving the earth, Jesus gave instructions for His disciples that are still in effect for us today.

Jesus came and spoke to them, saying, "All authority has been given to Me in heaven and on earth. Go therefore and make disciples of all nations, baptizing them in the name of the Father and of the Son and of the Holy Spirit, teaching them to observe all things that I have commanded you; and, lo, I am with you always, even to the end of the age."

MATTHEW 28:18–20 NKJV

As the earthly administrators of His heavenly kingdom, we are to teach, heal the sick, cast out devils, call for repentance, and live a holy and joy-filled life. This is a demonstration of the kingdom authority He gives us.

A Different View of Ourselves

What do we know about any king? Well, for one thing, a king isn't elected to office. He's born into his position. He rules those in his kingdom with absolute authority. A king never frets about paying his bills, or worries if there will be enough food to eat. Everything he wants is at his disposal, including the authority to use it. His kingdom will take on his attributes. The people will obey the king's laws, listen to and honor the king's message, and show absolute honor, respect, and admiration for the king. As they do, they will become *like him*. They will each be expressions of his kingdom.

Those who are hand chosen by the king to serve as his ambassadors do everything to symbolize the kingdom. His ambassadors don't proclaim their own message—they declare his. Scripture calls us "Christ's ambassadors" (2 Corinthians 5:20). That being true, we are to commit ourselves to our King's interests. We are paid and supported by the King. We are authorized by the King and protected by the resources of His kingdom. As His divine diplomats, Satan has no authority to fire us, disqualify us, or remove us from our ambassadorship. Our King has granted us a lifetime commission! However, if we fail to take advantage of the wonderful privilege to represent our King and His kingdom, we can certainly disqualify ourselves.

As a healthy child grows, he learns that his parents have other roles, relationships, and responsibilities. So also do growing Christians. We learn that our Father God has more things to do than simply meet our needs. He administers a kingdom and is vitally concerned for lost humanity. He's brokenhearted over the spiritual condition of our neighborhoods, cities, and nations.

When I was a young Christian, I lived with the fear that I was going to do something wrong, and God was going to *hurt me*. But the longer I know Him, the more I live with the fear that I'm going to do something that will *hurt Him*.

Similarly, when I was a young Christian I thought prayer was about me—my needs and my interests. As I've grown older, I've come to realize that prayer is really about God and His interests. Scripture says He's looking for two types of folks. He is looking for those who will worship Him in spirit and in truth (see John 4:23) and for those who will pray kingdom prayers (see Ezekiel 22:30). This is a divine partnership the Lord longs for us to enter into with Him.

Once we begin to receive this revelation and become kingdom-oriented, we graduate from need-centered praying to purpose-driven prayer. We realize that prayer has a higher purpose, to accomplish God's eternal agenda. When we begin praying in that direction, self begins to fade and Christ becomes Lord of our praying.

How about you? Have you been praying immature prayers, thinking that you are God's primary agenda? Have you thought of prayer only as a way to get your needs met? As we mature in Christ, we learn that prayer isn't primarily about us. It's about our Father, our Dad, who rules an eternal kingdom, and He has called us to join with Him in prayer— to expand the family business.

5

PRAYING *to a* CREATOR

I WALKED INTO an idol shop in Madras, India, one day. The owner was squatting on the floor in the corner, holding a log with his bare feet, while he chopped away with a sharp carving axe.

"What are you making?" I asked him.

He said, "I'm carving a god."

"Which god?"

He said the name of the god, a name I could never pronounce.

"What is this god's purpose?" I asked.

"It's the god of prosperity," he replied.

I replied frantically to his answer: "Hurry. Finish him. Quickly!"

"Why the rush?" he said, puzzled by my insistence.

"Look outside your shop. There are lepers lying beside

your doorway. There are beggars at the street corner. There is poverty everywhere. Quick! Finish carving this god of prosperity so he can go to work for them!"

I'll never forget the look on his face. It seemed to say, *"What you just said makes sense to me."*

Prayer is built into the hearts of everyone, whether their gods are represented by nature (i.e., the earth, sun, moon, stars, mountains, volcanoes) or are gods of their own making (idols). Paul tells us that idols are not gods at all. But the deceptive evil powers behind them are demonic spirits.

Christians do not pray to nature or to man-made gods. We pray to the God and Father of our Lord Jesus Christ, Jehovah, Creator of all things. But it is important that we know Him, if He is to hear us. I'm not only referring to knowing Him as Lord and Savior. I also mean knowing *who He is and what He is like.* I'm talking about knowing His intentions, His goals, His methods, and His procedures.

In Psalm 103:7 we read, "He [God] made known his ways to Moses, his deeds to the people of Israel." The Israelites learned God's deeds—*what* He did. But most of them never learned God's ways—*why* He did it. The deeds of God reveal God's *ability*; His ways reveal His *intentions*. This explains the difference between the way the children of Israel prayed and the way Moses prayed. To Moses, his relationship with God was to be cherished and nurtured. To the Israelites, God was little more than a "problem-solver." They never saw beyond their problems. They only knew *about* God, but Moses *knew* God!

TO WHOM DO WE PRAY?

The Bible is God's revelation of himself to us. In the study of Scripture there is what some call "the law of first-mention." Simply stated, the first mention of a thing in Scripture carries special significance. God first refers to himself in Scripture in Genesis 1:1. He said, "In the beginning God created. . . ." The Hebrew word used here for *created* means "to create something out of nothing." God isn't into duplication. He is a creator. God's middle name isn't Xerox (copier). Creativity is central to both how God sees and how He solves our problems.

God sees himself and wants us to see Him as "Creator." He is the only true creator. Every other "creation" is merely a rearrangement of what God has already produced. Neither Satan nor man can truly create. The following story makes my point.

A group of scientists got together and decided that man had evolved to the point that he no longer needed God. They chose one of their brightest to take the message to God that they were done with Him.

The scientist walked up to God and said, "God, we've arrived at the point that we can create life in a test tube, clone animals, and do many miraculous things. We've decided that we no longer need you. So why don't you just move along and mind your own business?"

God listened patiently to the man. When he finished talking, God said, "Very well. What do you say we have a 'man-making' contest?"

The scientist replied, "Sure, why not?"

God added, "And we'll do it just as I did with Adam in the garden of Eden."

"No problem," the self-assured scientist replied as he bent down and grabbed himself a handful of dirt.

God held out His hand and abruptly stopped him. "No sir," God said. "You get your own dirt."

SOME OF GOD'S CREATIVE RESPONSES

We should assume that when we make a request of God in prayer, He will answer us creatively. Consider some of His creative responses recorded in Scripture that Alice and I noted in our book *The Advocates:*

- *He caused a ram to be caught in a thicket.* Abraham was at the point of sacrificing his own son, Isaac, when he saw "a substitute" (Genesis 22:1–18).

- *He split the Red Sea.* Moses, with one million upset Israelites, was trapped on the banks of the Red Sea, and an entire Egyptian army was pursuing them (Exodus 14).

- *He sent a living submarine, a whale, for Jonah.* Jonah had resisted the call to evangelize Nineveh, when a large fish took him for a ride! (Jonah 1:12–2:10).

- *He caused an earthquake to effect a jailbreak.* Reread the story of Paul and Silas in prison in Acts 16, and you will notice that they weren't complaining that they had been beaten, nor were they looking for a way to escape. They weren't looking for a solution to their immediate problem. They knew the ways of God (His plan) and were focused on the God of their problem!

- *He sent pizza by delivery ravens.* Elijah had just declared a drought to the wicked King Ahab, and Ahab was mad. God told Elijah to go and hide (1 Kings 17:1–7).

- *He dropped down manna from heaven.* Moses' bunch was tired, hungry, and grumbling when God ordered a special delivery meal for them (Exodus 16:1–22).

- *He prescribed seven dips in a dirty river.* Naaman, a sophisticated military captain, had leprosy. His instruction from the prophet seemed ridiculous to him (2 Kings 5:1–14).

- *He used everyday things—"spit" and "mud."* A man had been blind from birth. He wanted to be healed. No doubt this is the source of the popular toast "Here's mud in your eye," which is another way of saying "Here's to your health" (John 9:1–38).[1]

Spit? Mud?! Yes. John describes a man who was born blind. Don't you imagine that he and others had prayed many times for his healing? But when Jesus' disciples asked whose sins were responsible for his blindness, Jesus answered, "Neither this man nor his parents sinned . . . but this happened so that the work of God might be displayed in his life" (John 9:3). What?! It's true. It was God who had formed a sightless baby in his mother's womb. Why? God did so because He had a purpose for the man's blindness. You see, there was more here than a blind baby. This man was "a miracle" waiting to happen! There was a divine purpose involved in his condition. To pray effectively for such a man would have required discovering and praying toward God's purpose.

This kind of revelatory knowledge is hard for American Christians to receive. Because we, unlike Christians in Sudan, Iran, Iraq, and many other places on the earth, are so pampered and protected that we think *God exists for us* . . . right?

Wrong. Although He loves us supremely, He is always focused on His purposes. To pray effectively, we must take God's purposes to heart.

PAUL UNDERSTOOD THE WAYS OF GOD

The experience of the apostle Paul provides us with another challenge along this line. In 2 Corinthians 12:7, we learn that Paul had a problem. He dubbed it "a thorn in his flesh" and "a messenger of Satan." He prayed three times for God to remove it. But three times God answered, "No." Why? God loved Paul. Why would God allow demonic torment to touch His faithful servant? Why would God reject Paul's requests for healing? Why did God say yes to the blind man in John 9, and no to Paul?

The prophet Isaiah gives us a clue. He writes in Isaiah 55:9, "As the heavens are higher than the earth, so are my ways higher than your ways and my thoughts than your thoughts." His ways are higher than our ways. It sounds strange to our limited thinking, but God healed one and not the other for the very same reason, which is the reason for everything God does—*for His glory*!

Paul knew, or came to know, why God chose not to heal him. He knew that it had to do with God's purposes. He knew:

- That God had told Moses, "But as truly as I live, all the earth shall be filled with the glory of the Lord" (Numbers 14:21 KJV).

- That Isaiah had written, "I am the Lord; that is my name! I will not give my glory to another" (Isaiah 42:8).

- That Jesus had said, "He that speaketh of himself seeketh his own glory" (John 7:18 KJV).

I suppose Paul concluded that if the whole earth is full of the glory of God, there is no place left for "the glory of Paul." So later he explained, "To keep me from becoming conceited because of these surpassingly great revelations, there was given me a thorn in my flesh, a messenger of Satan, to torment me" (2 Corinthians 12:7). Notice Paul says this issue or entity was "given" to him. I don't suppose we will ever fully understand this, but God couldn't have received as much glory in Paul's one-time healing as He did by presenting him to the world as a "wounded warrior," daily dependent upon God, yet graced to glorify Christ in the midst of hardship!

So Paul said, "Therefore I will boast all the more gladly about my weaknesses, so that Christ's power may rest on me" (v. 9). A man who is committed to God's purposes can boast of his infirmity. He is a man who has lost himself in God! Paul would rather have Christ's power than be healed. A man who arrives at a place where he can boast in his infirmity is a man committed to the purposes of God. Paul said, "Godliness with contentment is great gain" (see 1 Timothy 6:6). He also said, "I have learned to be content whatever the circumstances" (Philippians 4:11).

Our heavenly Father loves us. He is concerned about us. He wants to heal our bodies and solve our problems. He takes no delight in our suffering. But we are fallen beings with limited understanding, who live on a sin-cursed planet. God's kingdom has not yet fully come, which is why we pray, "Thy kingdom come. Thy will be done in earth, as it is in heaven" (Matthew 6:10 KJV). Sickness and death are yet to be done away with completely. He will never answer our prayers at the expense of accomplishing His purpose. God's purpose is to demonstrate His power, glorify His name, and extend His kingdom on the earth. And that's why we call Him *God*.

DREAMERS AND VISIONARIES

When there are tasks to be done and problems to be solved, we look to creators: writers, inventors, musicians, and artists. They are dreamers and visionaries. They conceptualize solutions to problems. They actually see the solutions before they exist. Beginning with a problem or task, they focus on finding a solution, and everything they do relates to that purpose. They work instinctively, don't particularly like structure, and are often frustrated by directions.

Creators are "pregnant" with ideas until their concepts become reality. During this process, they impart a bit of themselves in their products. God said, "So God created man in his own image, in the image of God he created him; male and female he created them" (Genesis 1:27). Without question, our mighty Creator answers our prayers creatively.

For example, we hired a company to extend the patio on our home. It was little more than a small slab of concrete at the time. When the designer came in, he sat down at our dining table and pulled out his portfolio (photos of past projects he'd designed), pen and paper. After opening pleasantries I said, "Let me explain what we'd like to do with our patio."

He grabbed his pen and paper and said, "I think I know what you want. You'd like to extend it in this direction and shape."

We said, "Yes, that's a good idea, and—"

He interrupted, "Then you want to . . ."

In five minutes he had designed the complete project—without our help, I might add. He didn't need our instructions or ideas. He gets paid to create, not take orders.

When we pray with "problem-solving" in mind, rather than make our plea to God as Creator, letting Him plan the solution, we often instruct God in our prayer. Such requests frustrate a creator!

Job tried instructing God. And in Job 38, God said (my paraphrase), "Job, why are you instructing me? Where were you when I created the world? I didn't need your help then. And I don't need your instructions now."

Think about this. When you pray, "God, please let me get that job," you are praying, "God, please do for me the thing I have already decided is best for me. I've done all the thinking; all you have to do, God, is copy me. I have it lined out: Give me the job." In so doing, you are appealing to God's *productive* side rather than His *creative* side. You're elevating "problem-solving" above God's higher purposes. You're instructing Him as to what you want and how you want it rather than trusting your loving Creator to demonstrate His power by accomplishing *His purpose* regarding you.

Can you see how this prayer in itself conflicts with the creative nature of God? You aren't asking Him to activate His unique plan for you. You are asking Him to *produce* for you that which you've already decided is best. So you're not praying to God as Creator. You're overlooking the fact that the Lord wants to creatively do things for you, things that are "exceedingly abundantly above all that we ask or think" (Ephesians 3:20 NKJV), or as Jeremiah wrote, "marvelous and wondrous things that you could never figure out on your own" (Jeremiah 33:3 THE MESSAGE).

Why are you giving God instructions? Why are you trying

to engage God in your plans and purposes, instead of recognizing that He has plans and purposes for you—plans that are far bigger than you realize?

Since God's response will be above what you can ask or think, something that you could never figure out on your own, what good are your instructions? Resist the urge to explain things to your omniscient God when you pray. Fight the urge to give Him directions as to how you want Him to solve your problems. Ask the Lord to show you the big picture! Learn *what* God does, and *why* and *how* He does it. Most of His intervention in history has been as a creator.

HOW TO KNOW GOD'S WILL

- *Abide in Him*. John 15:7 tells us that knowing the will of God is a result of abiding in Him and His words abiding in us. It is to live as a branch, attached to the Vine (Jesus), so that His life is our life, His thoughts are our thoughts, and so on. We become identified with Him. How do we know if we are "abiding in Him" in this way? Quite simply, here's how we know: A healthy branch, attached to a vine, receives nourishment from it and bears fruit!

- *Allow His words (God's Word) to abide in you*. You can't know God any better than you know His Word as revealed in Scripture.

- *Spend time in His presence*. It's hard to know the heart of a friend with whom you spend little time.

- *Ask Him*. Yes! We're talking about prayer, right? Then pray that God will reveal His will to you.

Sometimes He will; He'll show you what He's doing and what He's planned for you. The idea of asking God to reveal His will isn't new. As I've mentioned, Moses knew God's ways. We're told in Exodus 33:13 that he asked God to show him His ways. King David also prayed to know God's ways. In Psalm 25:4 (THE MESSAGE), he prayed, "Show me how you work, God; school me in your ways."

- Ask him for multiple confirmations. Scripture teaches the value of two or three witnesses to confirm a thing. (See Matthew 18:16; 2 Corinthians 13:1.) So ask God to provide unmistakable, multiple confirmations. There's nothing wrong with that. After all, it was His suggestion.

  Even if He doesn't reveal *the knowledge* of His will, pray that He will keep you in the center of it. Is that possible? Absolutely. The pilot of an airplane doesn't have to be able to see the airstrip, or even know exactly where he is, as long as he is in radio contact with the tower. The tower has the pilot on their radar. They know his altitude, location, direction, and speed of travel, and they will guide him to a safe landing.

  If you don't know "where you are today" in the context of God's will (His plan for your life), don't press Him for "the knowledge" of His will. Sometimes the Lord withholds the knowledge to teach us to walk by faith. Just as the pilot listens to the tower operator and places his faith in his or her instructions, so God asks us to do the same at times. Oddly, we may not know where we are, or where we're going, but we can still stay in the center of His will as we obediently follow His instructions.

As Jesus told His disciples, before teaching them the model prayer: "Your Father knows the things you have need of before you ask Him" (Matthew 6:8 NKJV). Resist the urge to explain things to God—He knows everything. Fight the urge to instruct Him or to explain how you want the Lord to solve your problem.

A GOD OF PURPOSE

My father taught me: "The man who knows *how* will always work for a man who knows *why*." We've seen that God works creatively. But *why* does God do what He does?

Why? *For His glory!* Everything that exists does so for a reason. John wrote, "You are worthy, O Lord, to receive glory and honor and power; for You created all things, *and by Your will they exist and were created*" (Revelation 4:11 NKJV, emphasis added).

Our problems are forever changing, but God's purposes remain the same. The psalmist wrote, "But the plans of the Lord stand firm forever, the purposes of his heart through all generations" (Psalm 33:11).

Alice's dad, football coach Gene Day, would close every prayer he prayed with the words "in Jesus' name *and for His sake*, I pray, amen." He's been with the Lord for years, but I can hear him saying it yet today. He added inflection in his voice, accenting the words *and for His sake*. But we don't hear the words *and for His sake* much anymore. What does this phrase mean exactly? It means that I am subjugating my prayer request to God's purposes—and for His sake. God has said,

"For my own sake, for my own sake, I do this" (Isaiah 48:11).

Two things trouble me about some Christians. One is that they seem to view themselves as the center of God's universe. Listening to them, you'd think that God exists to meet their needs. In fact, some churches are built on the basis of that "false gospel" message.

I heard a television pastor recently preach, "Friend, I know you're concerned about losing your job. But I want you to hold your head up and realize that there was a reason that you lost your job. And that reason was because God has got a *better job* waiting for you."

I was shocked and disgusted. How can he say that? Some of those people who lost their jobs lost them because they were lousy workers. They were fired because they took advantage of their bosses! But the purveyors of these "feel good, because you are the center of God's world" messages are doing nothing more than building egos and robbing people of a true understanding of God's ways.

Often the Lord reveals His purposes in us and through us, when we are engaged in spiritual warfare, so He can enlighten us and shame Satan and his minions. Paul writes, "To the intent that now the manifold wisdom of God might be made known by the church [us] to the principalities and powers in the heavenly places, [Satan and his demons] according to the eternal purpose [there it is!] which He accomplished in Christ Jesus our Lord" (Ephesians 3:10–11 NKJV). Simply put . . . God just loves to demonstrate His power!

Secondly, I'm troubled by those Christians who apparently feel that the devil works 24/7, devising plans to mess up their lives. But the truth is, as someone pointed out, "Some, who are concerned over what people think of them, might be surprised to find out how seldom people do." Some people might also be surprised to discover that they are not Satan's *primary enemy*. What do I mean?

Satan's Number One Enemy

Some Christians feel like they are the prime target of Satan's attacks. But Scripture does not teach this. Here are some important things to keep in mind about him and how he works:

- *First, Satan isn't omnipresent like God*, who is everywhere. Like us, the devil can only be at one place at a time. So he's most likely never laid eyes on us.

- *Second, he's not omniscient like God*, who knows all things. It's inconceivable to think that Satan even knows our individual names.

- *Third, Satan isn't omnipotent like God*, who can do anything. The devil's true enemy is our heavenly Father. Satan was at war with our Daddy for thousands of years before we came along.

Now, read carefully. This next section could change the way you've understood your Christian life. I've discovered only three things Satan can do to hurt his enemy—God.

- *First, Satan keeps people separated from God*. He knows that God is a father who wants a house full of kids. Because God created everyone to live with Him forever, the enemy blinds them from seeing the truth of the gospel. (See 2 Corinthians 4:3–4.) His goal? To rob God of His children. (See Isaiah 10:14.)

- *Second, Satan hurts us.* He hurts God by hurting us. When we hurt, God hurts. Alice and I have four precious children. When one of them hurts, we hurt. And if you hurt one of our children or grand-children, you've hurt us.

- *Third, Satan tempts us into doing things that hurt God.* If you're a parent, you know this is true. No one can hurt parents more than their children can. And no one can make them prouder. Why? Perhaps it's because children are extensions of their parents.

God's ways are above our ways. As we begin to realize this, we'll discover that we've wasted a lot of words instructing God and praying for things that He won't do because they conflict with His ultimate plan.

Rather than create our lists of requests determined by our needs, we ought to focus on *God, and what He's doing on the earth.* God has a purpose and a plan. Our job is to find out what they are and pray accordingly.

"What's God Doing in This City?"

I was teaching at a spiritual warfare conference in the northeast. At one point I asked, "Can anyone tell me what the devil's doing in this city?"

Hands flew into the air; many exuberantly jumped to their feet and cried, "I can, I can."

"Please be seated," I encouraged as I tried to regain some semblance of order.

"I'm really not concerned with what the devil is doing. Can any of you tell me what *God* is doing in this city?" I asked.

Suddenly the room grew silent. They cocked their heads to one side and looked at me quizzically with their brows furrowed, as if I were speaking Mandarin Chinese!

"Isn't it interesting?" I continued. "All of you can tell me ten things the devil's doing in your city, but you can't tell me what God is doing?" No one could.

As the bride of Christ, we are His "helpmeets" or helpmates. We are here to help Him do what He's doing. Jesus said that He only did what He saw the Father doing (John 5:19). He also said, "As the Father has sent me, I am sending you" (John 20:21). We are to serve on the same basis. If we haven't bothered to identify what God is doing, how can we help Him do it? How would we know the first thing to do? Can we conclude, then, that what the devil is doing is most often directing our prayer lives?

Sadly, in many (if not most) cases, it is. We are engaged in the ritual of finding problems Satan has caused and praying for God to solve them. Indeed, we seem to view ourselves as "God's troubleshooters." We've lost all sight of God, His activity, His glory, and His kingdom!

SUPERSTITION OR TRUTH?

Alice and I are increasingly concerned with the level of prayer in the American church that is based more on superstition than truth. To some of us, prayer has been reduced to little more than spiritual damage control rather than being used to extend God's kingdom, accomplish His purposes, establish His lordship, and unleash damage to the prince of darkness. It's reactive prayer rather than proactive prayer.

God has two overriding purposes:

- First, the glory of His name. (See Exodus 3:15; 9:16; Malachi 1:11.)

- Second, the establishment and extension of His kingdom. (See Psalm 145:11–13; Habakkuk 2:14; Matthew 6:10.)

Rest assured that anything God does for you, in answer to your prayer, will be done in accordance with these two primary goals.

Illustrated in Egypt

After four hundred years of servitude to the Egyptians, Pharaoh granted the Israelites permission to leave. They had no more than begun their exodus when Pharaoh suddenly changed his mind and assembled his troops, and soon the world's greatest army (of that day) was hot on the heels of the Israelites.

God told the Israelites to encamp near the sea. "Then the Lord said to Moses, 'Tell the Israelites to turn back and encamp near Pi Hahiroth, between Migdol and the sea. They are to encamp by the sea, directly opposite Baal Zephon'" (Exodus 14:1–2).

The Israelites were confused by God's instruction to make camp by the sea. To encamp by the sea when an enemy is barreling down on you is not only poor military logic, it even defies common sense. After all, with your back to the sea, there's no way of escape. You're trapped!

God did go on to explain His reasons: "Pharaoh will think, 'The Israelites are wandering around the land in confusion, hemmed in by the desert.' And I will harden Pharaoh's heart, and he will pursue them" (Exodus 14:3–4). But I doubt that Moses got it. *Excuse me! God, what do you mean?*

Let's summarize. Facing certain annihilation, God's "favorite people" have been given unusual instructions: You camp out in the open where Pharaoh's army can find you, over there by the sea will be fine (v. 2); and I will harden Pharaoh's heart and he will pursue you (v. 4).

Don't you imagine their hearts sank when they heard God say, "I will harden Pharaoh's heart and he will pursue you"? Imagine yourself under those circumstances. Had I been there, I'd likely have assumed that it was the devil talking to me.

I would have prayed two "desperately anointed" prayers: "God, pleeeeze soften Pharaoh's heart," or . . . "God, we need one more plague. The 'river to blood plague' was awesome! But we need a major plague now. Not flies, not frogs—we need an *amazing* plague, God!"

Why would I pray that way? Because, perhaps like you, I tend to pray according to my knowledge and my past experiences. When I feel trapped, I tend to offer God instructions.

But God was through sending plagues on Egypt. He was about to do "exceedingly, abundantly, above all" that He had done before—actually split the Red Sea! And He definitely wasn't about to *soften* Pharaoh's heart. He was going to *harden* Pharaoh's heart, so he'd be lured by his own rage into the middle of the sea and drown. In Exodus 14:4 God says, "I will gain glory for myself through Pharaoh and all his army, and the Egyptians will know that I am the Lord." (See also Exodus 14:17–18.)

Isn't this an amazing picture of what we've been talking about? The Israelites were hemmed in between the devil and the deep blue sea, facing annihilation, and what was on God's mind? Their plight? Their problem? Sure. God knew their predicament. But above their circumstances, His thoughts were focused on His own glory! He was not going to answer them to solve their problem, but to accomplish His purpose.

Here it is. God said, "I will gain glory for myself through Pharaoh and all his army." How? How did He gain glory in this? "The people feared the Lord and put their trust in him" (Exodus 14:31).

The Israelites were focused on their immediate and rather serious problem; they were not focused on God's purpose. "Mountain-moving faith" sees beyond the horizon. It sees what others cannot see. (See Matthew 17:20.) We need to look beyond our problems to see His plans! Scripture is full of this truth.

- **"Now faith is being sure of what we hope for and certain of what we do not see. . . . By faith Noah, when warned about things not yet seen, in holy fear built an ark to save his family" (Hebrews 11:1, 7).**

- **Paul wrote, "So we fix our eyes not on what is seen, but on what is unseen. For what is seen is temporary, but what is unseen is eternal" (2 Corinthians 4:18).**

Insight, a Product of Intimacy

When we embrace God's plan with spiritual eyes of faith, we will be more committed to God's glory than to our success, and His purposes will supersede our problems.

Moses, exercising mountain-moving faith, told the people: "Do not be afraid. Stand firm and you will see the deliverance the Lord will bring you today. The Egyptians you see today you will never see again. The Lord will fight for you; you need only to be still" (Exodus 14:13–14).

Do you see it? There was no way the Israelites could know that in advance. It was above all that they could ask or think! (See Ephesians 3:20.) Had they offered God their instructions, they would have only frustrated the Creator, and missed His plan.

But Moses was different. He shared an intimacy with God in prayer that the other Israelites didn't even understand. In the midst of the national panic, God revealed His specific purposes to Moses. So he didn't respond by praying about his immediate problem, but was able to see beyond—to God's ultimate plan!

It's time for us to move from problem-centered to purpose-driven, kingdom-oriented prayer. Natural sight can see the mountains on the horizon. But "faith sight" can move mountains and see beyond the horizon! God wants us to see the plans and become His purposeful prayer partners!

I've been working with a man whose marriage is shaken. His wife's affection for him is in question, and he has frantically tried to repair their relationship. He's desperate for an answer. Yesterday he told me, "The Lord said that one of my problems is that I feel it's my job to fix this situation."

It can be difficult for some of us, as Moses told the Israelites, to "be still, stand firm, and trust God to fight for us." It's especially true when our world crumbles around us. But it's God's way of getting us to the place where we lose all faith in ourselves and trust Him alone.

In the account in Exodus 14, we see that God sent a cloud of separation, like a curtain. It created darkness on one side (where the Egyptians were) and light on the other (where

God was leading the Israelites). We too will experience these kinds of glorious manifestations if we will wait on His leading and obey His specific word to us.

> *Then Moses stretched out his hand over the sea, and all that night the Lord drove the sea back with a strong east wind and turned it into dry land. The waters were divided, and the Israelites went through the sea on dry ground, with a wall of water on their right and on their left.*
>
> *The Egyptians pursued them, and all Pharaoh's horses and chariots and horsemen followed them into the sea. During the last watch of the night the Lord looked down from the pillar of fire and cloud at the Egyptian army and threw it into confusion.*
>
> EXODUS 14:21–24

More creativity! The Egyptians were thrown into confusion and followed the Israelites into what was, for them, a sea of death.

Speaking of creativity, here is one of my favorite Bible verses: "He [God] *made the wheels of their chariots come off* so that they had difficulty driving" (v. 25, emphasis added). Did you say, "difficulty driving"? No kidding. It's hard enough to drive a *two-wheeled* chariot in the sand. A chariot without wheels is a sled!

Other than the humor, why is this verse a favorite of mine? It's because who among us would have thought to pray: "And, God, would you kindly remove the wheels from their chariots?" God's ways just aren't our ways. Since we can't even imagine how He will accomplish what He's promised to do, we'd best not be instructing Him.

And Pharaoh's army said, "Let's get away from the Israelites! The Lord is fighting for them against Egypt" (Exodus

14:25). That's the smartest thing they've come up with so far, don't you think? Finally Pharaoh was beginning to see the light. But he was, as we say in Texas, "a day late and a dollar short!"

Are you getting it? God is going to deliver His people, but His response isn't primarily about them—it's about Him! Moses raised the staff, and the sea split. You know, you saw the movie. And millions of Israelites took their animals and their possessions and walked across on dry ground. That's creative!

> Then the Lord said to Moses, "Stretch out your hand over the sea so that the waters may flow back over the Egyptians and their chariots and horsemen." Moses stretched out his hand over the sea, and at daybreak the sea went back to its place. The Egyptians were fleeing toward it, and the Lord swept them into the sea. The water flowed back and covered the chariots and horsemen—the entire army of Pharaoh that had followed the Israelites into the sea. Not one of them survived.
> EXODUS 14:26–28

Talk about an undertow! I'd say that was a "red flag day" at the beach! And as God had promised them in verse 13, their enemies disappeared that day and were swept to the bottom of the sea!

Paul reminded us, thousands of years later, "For the Scripture says to Pharaoh: 'I raised you up for this very purpose, that I might display my power in you and that my name might be proclaimed in all the earth'" (Romans 9:17). And today, thousands of years later, the Jews still tell the story of Pharaoh's defeat and God's glory!

> But the Israelites went through the sea on dry ground, with a wall of water on their right and on their left. That

day the Lord saved Israel from the hands of the Egyptians,
and Israel saw the Egyptians lying dead on the shore.
And when the Israelites saw the great power the Lord dis-
played against the Egyptians, the people feared the Lord
and put their trust in him and in Moses his servant.
EXODUS 14:29–31

The Israelites were no longer focusing on their problem, or even their solution. They were focusing on their Creator! In their exuberance, they sang the first praise song ever recorded in God's Word. You can read it in Exodus 15.

And the Egyptians, what were they thinking? We're not told. But you can be sure that word reached Egypt, and the Egyptians were stunned to hear about the demise of Pharaoh and his army. You can bet they knew that Jehovah was God of the heaven and the earth!

REVIVAL PRAYING IN TINY, TEXAS

Everything, including you and what you own, exists for God's purpose. *Problem-centered praying* identifies problems and forms requests with the goal of getting God involved. But *purpose-driven prayer* discovers what God is doing and forms requests appropriate to His purposes. Jesus said, "I tell you the truth, the Son can do nothing by himself; he can do only what he sees his Father doing, because whatever the Father does the Son also does" (John 5:19).

For example, suppose there were a town called Tiny, Texas, and that it had ten churches. And imagine that First Church was the recipient of a real, bona fide revival. Praying people are excited to see genuine revival, so they would swarm First Church like fire ants at a picnic!

Now, what would they pray once they got there? Quite simply, they'd pray for the other nine churches in town to experience the revival. I can almost hear them crying, *"O God, we won't rest until this revival sweeps every church in town. God, when are you going to move on our behalf? Can't you see that we have nine other churches here in need of revival? How long are we going to have to cry out before you revive them?"*

Sounds good, doesn't it? How selfless and generous of them. But there's a huge problem here. Look carefully at their prayer. And as you do, remember that *Jesus did only what He saw the Father doing.*

Instead of partnering with God by acknowledging and celebrating Him for who He is and what He's doing, they are ignoring what God is doing at First Church and are trying to persuade God to send revival to the other nine churches, something that is *their agenda*! They're giving God instructions!

We should spend more time identifying and blessing what God *is* doing. Don't you think if those wonderful people were to gather at First Church to celebrate and praise Jehovah for what He is doing, that He'd be more apt to do more? Certainly He would.

Ask yourself, "When I pray for someone or something, do I begin with what I see God doing or with what I *wish* He were doing?" May I suggest that you begin to:

- *Identify what God is doing.* What evidence, even subtle changes, do you see?

- *Thank God and praise Him for what He's doing.* Thank Him for the circumstances He is arranging, the people and the influences He is using, and the miracles He is performing in the situation.

- *Proclaim His works.* Glorify His name. Celebrate Him!

- *Ask Him to enlarge the area of His activity.* Ask Him to demonstrate His power and to glorify His name as He extends His kingdom in this matter.

What is your problem today? Have you considered His purposes in your problem and begun to pray accordingly? God wants to do more than provide your solution. He wants to demonstrate His miraculous, creative power, which will result in His name being glorified and His kingdom being extended. Invite God to fulfill His purposes in solving your problems, which will result in His glory!

Our greatest effectiveness in prayer begins when, as a result of our intimacy with Him, we learn His ways and pray accordingly. From now on, when you pray, expect that His solution will be creative. Don't offer the Creator instructions or lecture Him! Expect something new. Remind Him of His Word, ask Him for His purposes to be accomplished, and then prepare yourself for the unexpected!

> Live for something, have a purpose,
> And that purpose keep in view;
> Drifting like a helpless vessel
> You can never to life be true.
>
> Half the wrecks that strew life's ocean,
> If some star had been their guide,
> Might have now been safely riding,
> But they drifted with the tide.
> —Author Unknown

Rejoice, friend! Your dilemma today is God's opportunity to demonstrate and display His miraculous, creative power! (See James 1:2.)

So when you pray, expect your Creator to answer you creatively, do a new thing, carry out His purposes, and glorify His name in the answer.

6

WORRY-FILLED PRAYER

IN HIS 1988 hit song "Don't Worry, Be Happy," Bobby McFerrin, a preacher's kid, encouraged us not to let life's negative experiences get us down. It's not always easy to put Bobby's advice into practice, of course! Surprisingly to some, worry has a very direct link to prayer. Why, you ask? It's because anxiety and prayer are two great opposing forces that simply cannot cooperate. Consider this. Worry is unnecessary, impractical, and crippling to your prayer life.

One of my favorite sayings is: "Prayer is the ability to listen to the music of the future. Faith is the courage to dance to it today." This is why worriers have a hard time praying effectively. They are so focused on potential problems facing them that they can't hear the music of the future. And they are so fearful of all that may go wrong, they are not inclined to dance either!

Jesus certainly knew the importance of faith in our prayer life. Over and over He expressed disappointment in His disciples' lack of faith. (See Matthew 6:30; 8:26; 14:31; 16:8; Mark 4:40; Luke 12:28.) He told the blind men who wanted Him to heal them, "'According to your faith will it be done to you'" (Matthew 9:29). The writer to the Hebrews restates this vital connection between prayer and faith in God when he writes: "Without faith it is impossible to please God, because anyone who comes to him must believe that he exists and that *he rewards those who earnestly seek him*" (Hebrews 11:6, emphasis added).

Let's face it. Worry is something that we need to deal with, not just gloss over and excuse, because its effects are so negative on us. Jesus took this issue so seriously that He devoted a whole section of His Sermon on the Mount to it. Listen carefully to what He says.

> *Therefore I tell you,* do not worry *about your life, what you will eat; or about your body, what you will wear. Life is more than food, and the body more than clothes. Consider the ravens: They do not sow or reap, they have no storeroom or barn; yet God feeds them. And how much more valuable you are than birds! Who of you by* worrying *can add a single hour to his life? Since you cannot do this very little thing, why do you worry about the rest?*
>
> *Consider how the lilies grow. They do not labor or spin. Yet I tell you, not even Solomon in all his splendor was dressed like one of these. If that is how God clothes the grass of the field, which is here today, and tomorrow is thrown into the fire, how much more will he clothe you, O you of little faith! And do not set your heart on what you will eat or drink;* do not worry about it. *For the*

*pagan world runs after all such things, and your Father
knows that you need them. But seek his kingdom, and
these things will be given to you as well. Do not be
afraid, little flock, for your Father has been pleased to
give you the kingdom. . . . Where your treasure is,
there your heart will be also.*
  LUKE 12:22–34, EMPHASIS ADDED

WHAT IS WORRY, AND WHY DO WE WORRY?

Worry, Like Fear, Is Misplaced Trust

One of Satan's principal strategies is to arrange conditions
in our lives that will provoke anxiety (or worry). Why does
he do that? One reason is to embarrass Father God. Imagine
how God must feel when His own children question His
intentions or doubt His ability! Another reason is to sabotage
our praying. Our doubt-filled prayers will not be answered.
(See James 1:7–8.) So the first step toward effective prayer is
not to worry.

You see, worry isn't a failure to trust. It's actually misplaced trust. It isn't a lack of faith. It's faith in the wrong
thing! Sadly, a worrier has more faith in the enemy's threats
than in the Father's promises.

Corrie ten Boom (whose Dutch family hid Jews from
the Nazis during World War II, until all of her family—
except Corrie—died in German concentration camps)
spent the last two years of her life in Pastor Charles Swindoll's Fullerton, California, congregation. Dr. Swindoll
said, "It was a wonderful experience to have this godly
woman in our midst during that extended period of time as
we literally watched her die. She said on one occasion,

'Worry does not empty tomorrow of its sorrows; it empties today of its strength.'"[1]

A Christian who chronically worries may have had faith enough for *salvation*, but he's lacking faith for *sanctification*. He's like some of Moses' followers, whom God chastised because they did not profit from the lessons of the desert and mix faith with what they heard and saw from God. (See Hebrews 4:1–2; Jude 1:5.) Miss Ten Boom knew that worry is emotional poison.

Society Promotes Worry

Our worried culture depends on alcohol and drugs, both legal and illegal, to make it through the day. Some Christians are good at singing "Standing on the Promises," or the worship chorus "My Hope Is in You, Lord," while they pop pills for their anxiety in an attempt to resolve their emotional issues.

Stress causes worry, and worry causes stress. In some cases, worry is the result of our taking on responsibilities that God has not assigned to us.

It is reported that stress is the most common health problem reported by women. But men suffer from it as well. It will eventually register on your face and be revealed in your posture. Learn to deal with stress in both the big and the small things of your life.

Did you know that you can *worry yourself sick*? It's true. Worry is like an infection in the mind. It pollutes your thinking, misshapes your attitudes, tarnishes your conversations, and affects your decisions. Worry is the polluted soil in which the toxic seeds of depression germinate. And once those weeds of depression sprout and begin to bloom in the garden of your heart, they will eventually sap it of all hope. Serious? You bet it's serious. Left unchecked, depression will open the door to a "spirit of heaviness" (an evil spirit; see Isaiah 61:3 NKJV), which will lead to a life of misery and despair. When you see worry for what it is, you will begin to hate it like God hates it.

Worriers either sleep too much (to escape their worry), or not enough (because they are worried). Either brings on further maladies. Worry drives some people to overeat (obesity), while it drives others to starvation. Worry is a cruel taskmaster.

Creativity, like writing this book, requires a positive atmosphere. When a business needs a new product or concept, leaders typically assign that job to a creative team. I've served as a creative marketing consultant to various businesses through the years. During brainstorming sessions it's the rule (or general understanding) that anyone can offer a creative idea, regardless of what it is, but no one is allowed to critique any of the ideas that are presented. Why? It's because the brain cannot create and critique simultaneously. Your creative and critiquing mental functions do not co-operate. In the same way, like oil and water, worry and creativity are also mutually exclusive.

We are saddened to see someone bound to a wheelchair, physically paralyzed. But we don't realize that people can also be emotionally crippled. Eventually worry will paralyze a person mentally and emotionally. Like a dripping faucet, in time it will sap you of energy and reduce your body's ability to fight off diseases. It will cause hypertension (high blood pressure), nervous disorders, and much more.

Death was walking toward a city one morning when he met a man who asked, "Death, what are you here to do?"

"I've come to take 100 people," Death replied.

"That's horrible!" the man said.

"That's the way it is," Death explained. "That's what I do."

The man hurried to warn everyone he could about Death's plan. As evening fell he met Death again, leaving the city. "Death," he said. "You told me you were going to take 100 people. Why then did 1,000 die today?"

"I kept my word," Death responded. "I only took 100 people. Worry took the others."

—Author Unknown

Allow me to bottom-line it for you. Worry has no place in a believer's life. Whatever life throws our way, we can rest assured:

- "His [God's] divine power has given us everything we need for life and for godliness" (2 Peter 1:3).

- We truly "are complete in Him, who is the head of all principality and power" (Colossians 2:10 NKJV).

- "God will meet all your [our] needs according to his glorious riches in Christ Jesus" (Philippians 4:19).

God's remedy for overcoming worry is for us to "not be drunk with wine" (not be chemically dependent), but to be "filled with the Spirit . . . singing and making melody in your heart to the Lord" (Ephesians 5:18–19 NKJV). He recommends that we put on "the garment of praise for the spirit of heaviness" (Isaiah 61:3 NKJV).

Worry Is Often a Misplaced Sense of Responsibility

Some might ask, "Why shouldn't I worry? After all, when something goes wrong in my life, isn't it the height of irresponsibility for me not to worry? It's the mature, responsible thing to do, isn't it?" It may be the *natural* thing to do, but it is neither mature nor responsible. It is wrong. Worrying has never solved a problem. God says in Philippians 4:6 that we're not to worry or "be anxious about anything." The King James version uses the old English phrase, "be careful for nothing." But we need to keep in mind that being *careful for nothing* doesn't mean that we're to be *careless and irresponsible.*

Some worry over the consequence of their own actions. For example, they spend thousands of dollars more than they should on a new automobile, only to worry about how they are going to make the payments. This "homemade" worry has no place in a Christian's life.

Exercising responsibility means to care for things within our control. Godly stewardship requires that we take care of our responsibilities and give attention to duty.

Perhaps you heard about the lady sitting beside the minister on the plane. Suddenly the plane hit some turbulence and began to vibrate violently. Stricken with fear, the lady, thinking that the minister might have an inside connection with God, turned to him and said, "Reverend, isn't there something you can do?" The minister said, "No ma'am. I'm in sales, not management."

Let's not confuse worry with legitimate concern. Concern acknowledges a problem, then takes the steps necessary to correct it. Worry recognizes a problem, and then runs around in circles, fretting, not thinking, not taking action, and not trusting God with the outcome. As Zig Ziglar puts it, "Worry is interest paid on trouble before it's due."

Do you see it? Worry is more than a character flaw, a bad habit, or a "family trait." Worry is sin. Since the wages of any sin is death, worry pollutes everything it touches. It's self-centered and counterproductive. Worry is "a darkroom" in which life's negatives are developed. Bill Gothard, president of the Institute in Basic Life Principles, says, "Worry is accepting responsibility that was never yours in the first place."[2]

Jesus knew that we would most likely feel responsible for the basic needs of life, things like food and clothing. So He addressed those very things in His teachings about the birds and the flowers. Worry is the tendency to move *away from trusting God* to trusting ourselves and others. A person with good intentions feels the responsibility to keep things on course, to control circumstances and situations. Gradually, his need to control things becomes a need to control people. The struggle to control others creates tension and turmoil, which exacerbates worry. We don't help God manage our lives by fretting and complaining.

A final point needs to be made in this discussion about a misplaced sense of responsibility. On some occasions a person can go to the other extreme. He can begin to neglect his true responsibilities and expect God to do what he himself should be doing. To understand this, take a look at Jim.

Jim, a husband and father, has been unemployed for the past three years. He has quit the job search, however. Rather than take a job that would enable him to at least contribute something to the support of his family, Jim excuses himself by saying, "I'm just going to wait in prayer for the Lord to open the right door and provide me with my ideal job."

It would signal faith if Jim were to diligently work one, or even two menial jobs, to see his family's needs met while he waits for God to provide his "ideal job." Instead, by choosing not to work, Jim is not exercising faith; he's operating in presumption. The line between faith and presumption is often thin and blurry. Jim is certainly carefree concerning his joblessness. He's definitely not worried. But he is irresponsible. And both worry and irresponsibility are wrong in God's eyes.

As the familiar *Serenity Prayer* suggests, we need God's wisdom to discern the difference between those things that we can and cannot change. Then we need the serenity (the quiet patience) to accept those things we cannot change and the courage and personal discipline to change the things we can.

Worry Is Refusing to Live in "the Now"

Think about this. Worry is either a preoccupation with the past or with the future. A worrier is focusing either on what did or did not happen in the past, or on what may or may not happen in the future. So why is that a *problem*?

To understand why this is a problem we should remember the name God gave himself, when speaking to Moses. He chose the name "I AM." (See Exodus 3:14.) In other words, He is "a now God," to whom everything is always *present tense*. Why does the Bible say in Ephesians 2:4–7 that we are (present tense) seated together with Christ in the heavenly places? Because in God's heart and mind, that's where we are! He's enjoying us there *now*. Living in the past or the future is contrary to the nature of God. He's the God of the now!

People who anticipate that things will probably turn out badly are called pessimists. These worriers choose to focus on their disappointing past or an uncertain future. I love optimistic people—people who see the good in others and figure that things will turn out okay by the grace of God. Have you heard the story of the optimistic man who fell off of a forty-story building? As he passed a thirtieth-floor window he was heard to say, "So far, so good!"

My friend Jimmy Draper tells a funny story about his remarkably optimistic mother. One day he said, "Mother, you never have a negative word to say about anyone. I don't think you'd even have a negative word to say about the devil."

"Well, son," she said, "you must admit, he does stick to his job."

Worry dishonors God. How? By calling into question His integrity! Worry questions whether He means what He has said or whether He can do what He's promised. Since our faith enables God to do what He does on earth, faith is the "currency" of heaven. That means worriers and pessimists are nearing spiritual "bankruptcy." That's a bad place to be! Worriers are rarely happy with themselves. Having lost their faith in God, they quickly lose faith in others, and they will ultimately lose faith in themselves.

WARRIORS VS. WHINERS

Are you a winner or a whiner? Do you remember the "Whiner family" from the early days of the *Saturday Night*

Live television show? Have you ever had a friend who was a whiner? Whiners somehow manage to hijack every conversation and refocus it on themselves, attempting to drag anyone who'll listen through every minute detail of their lives.

Sadly, whiners seem to think they are the only people on earth with problems, and that the rest of the world needs to hear their current list. Worriers and whiners will never be warriors and winners!

You see, circumstances don't produce the attitudes of worriers and whiners—they reveal them. *New Science Magazine* reported a world values survey that analyzed the levels of happiness in more than sixty-five countries. Of the nations surveyed, the United States ranked sixteenth on the list, even though the standard of living in the U.S. far exceeds that of the fifteen happiest nations. Regardless of our being the most blessed people in history and the most blessed people on the planet, we still have an insatiable desire for more stuff. It's harder and harder to find a contented Christian, even though Paul said, "I have learned, in whatsoever state I am, therewith to be content" (Philippians 4:11 KJV). Paul told Timothy, "Godliness with contentment is great gain" (1 Timothy 6:6). Never forget: Happiness doesn't make us grateful. Gratitude makes us happy.

There was once a village water well in which hung two well-buckets tied to opposite ends of the same rope. When one bucket was drawn up filled with water, the other bucket would be let down to retrieve water. The strange thing about these well-buckets was that one of them was always happy, while the other was always sad.

Finally, one day the happy bucket stopped the sad bucket midway in the well and said, "I need to ask you something. You and I work in the same well, we travel the same distance, and we carry the same water. We share exactly the same circumstances. I am always joyful, but you are always sad. Why?"

The sad bucket thought for a moment and then replied, "Well, it seems that no matter how full I come up, I always go down empty."

The joyful bucket shook his head in disbelief, smiled, and said, "Not me. The way I see it, no matter how empty I go down, I always come up full!"

Which well-bucket are you? A worrier's glass is always half empty. What about you? Is your glass half empty or half full? Not sure? I assure you, your family and others closest to you know whether you are a worrier or a prayer warrior. If necessary, ask them.

THE WORRY TEST

Okay, it's time for a test. Allow me to put the "stethoscope of truth" to your life, check the level of your faith, and see how worry affects your life.

Take this little test and see if worry is hindering your prayer life and preventing you from living victoriously in Christ.

Give yourself a "1" for *rarely*, a "2" for *sometimes*, and a "3" for *often*.

_____ 1. Are you concerned with "what if . . .?"
_____ 2. Do you anticipate the worst?
_____ 3. Does your concern interfere with your life and daily routine?
_____ 4. Are you irritable, restless, and constantly on edge?

_____ 5. Do you have difficulty falling asleep, or sleeping through the night?

_____ 6. Do people ask what's bothering you?

_____ 7. When something good happens, do you assume the next thing that happens will be bad?

_____ 8. When opening your mail, do you look for bad news?

_____ 9. When the phone rings, do you wonder what's wrong?

_____ 10. Do those who know you best say you worry too much?

_____ Now total your score.

10–15: Good. You enjoy life and focus on the positives.

16–20: You worry more than you should.

21–30: Worry is a primary hindrance in your life.

Whatever your score, are you willing to abandon worry? Okay. Let's get to it!

GOD'S PRESCRIPTION FOR OVERCOMING WORRY

Don't worry about anything, but pray about everything. With thankful hearts offer up your prayers and requests to God. Then, because you belong to Christ Jesus, God will bless you with peace that no one can completely understand. And this peace will control the way you think and feel.

PHILIPPIANS 4:6–7 CEV

There are several prescriptions that won't cure worry.

You say, "I've tried taking my thoughts captive and bringing them into obedience to Christ" or "I've rebuked the devil for years over this issue."

Paul's statement about "taking thoughts captive" in 2 Corinthians 10:5 is about confronting men's philosophies and false doctrine with God's truth. Taking thoughts captive, according to Paul, has to do with how we, in the power of the Holy Spirit and truth, *persuade others* to abandon Satan's lies and embrace God's truth.

Here is the problem as I see it. A worrier (one who believes the enemy's lies) cannot take his anxiety-ridden thoughts captive (with his worried mind) and make them obey Christ. It's like wrestling with a pig. The only thing that happens when one wrestles a pig is that they both get muddy. Although perfectly true, taken in context this verse simply isn't the solution for worry.

Rebuke the devil? Why would you rebuke the devil? He's not the worrier—you are! When you stand before Christ's judgment seat, you can't use the devil or his demons as an excuse for the time and energy you wasted worrying. You are accountable for the life you choose to live.

Okay, if these strategies don't work, what does? Let's look at *God's prescription* for worry: *Praying with thanksgiving*. When you pray with thanksgiving, you get this amazing "worry-killing" promise: "God will bless you with peace that no one can completely understand. And this peace will control the way you think and feel." Voila! No more worry! Here's how *The Message* puts this awesome promise in Philippians 4:6–7: "Don't fret or worry. Instead of worrying, pray. Let petitions and praises shape your worries into prayers, letting God know your concerns. Before you know it, *a sense of God's wholeness, everything coming together for good, will come and settle you down.*

It's wonderful what happens when Christ displaces worry at the center of your life" (emphasis added).

In order to overcome worry you have to bring everything that affects your life before the Lord in prayer: your wants, your needs, and those of your family. Especially bring distressing things like afflictions, embarrassments, and trials—things that others worry about. Spread out before Him anything pertaining to body, mind, friends, family, conflicts, losses, trials, hopes, and fears. Present the secular and the sacred to Him, because as far as God is concerned, nothing about you is secular!

Don't think I'm contradicting what I told you earlier. In chapter 4, for example, I suggested that you shift your focus in prayer from your *own needs* to *kingdom issues*. The reason I'm saying this now, in this chapter, is because until you gain victory over worry you can't move up to more mature praying. Worry is a serious hindrance to us as God's children, and He wants us freed from it. That happens when we take the things that matter to us to Him *with thanksgiving.* When we do that, worry will supernaturally fade away and we can turn our attention to more kingdom-centered prayer.

Praise Is a Sacrifice

If you tend to worry, I want to remind you of something. No matter what storm you are in today, there is a cleft in the rock. God has prepared a shelter for you in the time of storm. But don't miss this. It isn't a shelter *from* the storm. It's a shelter *in* the storm! I call it "a divine disconnect." It's the amazing ability to have a broken heart, a peaceful mind, and the joy of the Lord—while the storm is (sometimes) still raging!

Saturate your requests with thanksgiving—praise! Thank God in advance for doing what you're asking Him to do. You may be thinking, *What if I don't really* feel like *praising? I've been quite depressed lately.* Then stand to your feet, throw your shoulders back, lift up your head, and praise Him anyhow! It's to be *a sacrifice* of praise (see Hebrews 13:15 NKJV). Praise Him *until* you feel like it. The hardest thing to do is to begin. The second hardest thing to do will be to stop once you start. You were born to praise Him! King David said he would never offer God a sacrifice that cost him nothing. Something has to die in order to produce a sacrifice—and you are the sacrifice.

Louise Redden, a poorly dressed lady with a look of defeat on her face, walked into a grocery store. She approached the owner of the store in a most humble manner and asked if he would let her charge a few groceries. She softly explained that her husband was very ill and unable to work, they had seven children, and they needed food.

John Longhouse, the grocer, scoffed at her and requested that she leave his store. Visualizing the family needs, she said, "Please, sir! I will bring you the money just as soon as I can." John told her he could not give her credit, as she did not have a charge account at his store.

Standing beside the counter was a customer who overheard the conversation between the two. The customer walked forward and told the grocer that he would stand good for whatever she needed for her family. The grocer said in a very reluctant voice, "Do you have a grocery list?"

Louise replied, "Yes, sir."

"Okay," he said, "put your grocery list on the scales. Whatever your grocery list weighs, I will give you that amount in groceries." Louise hesitated a moment with a bowed head, then she reached into her purse, took out a piece of paper, and scribbled something on it. She laid the piece of paper on the scale carefully with her head still bowed.

The grocer and customer were amazed when the scales went down and stayed down. The grocer, staring at the scales, turned slowly to the customer and said begrudgingly, "I can't believe it." The customer smiled, and the grocer started putting the groceries on the other side of the scales. The scale did not balance, so he put more and more groceries on them until the scales would hold no more.

The grocer stood there in utter disgust. Finally, he grabbed the piece of paper from the scales and looked at it with greater amazement. It was not a grocery list, but a prayer that read, "Dear Lord, you know my needs, and I am leaving this in your hands."

The grocer gave her the groceries that he had placed on the scales and stood in stunned silence. Louise thanked him and left the store.

The customer handed a fifty-dollar bill to John as he said, "It was worth every penny of it." It was sometime later that John Longhouse discovered the scales were broken; therefore, only God knows how much a prayer weighs.

—Author Unknown

GOD'S PROMISE

Your heavenly Father already knows all of your needs, and He will give you all you need from day to day if you live for Him and make the kingdom of God your primary concern.

MATTHEW 6:32–33, MY PARAPHRASE

Read that verse carefully. There are some salient points to remember that will help you win over worry and pray more effectively.

1. God already knows all your needs. Mention them to Him. No need to explain anything to an omniscient God.
2. He will give you all you need from day to day. Praise Him for it *now*, even though you can't see it.
3. But remember, God's promises are conditional. You must do your part if you expect God to do His part. What's your part?
   a. Live for Him.
   b. Make His kingdom your primary concern. Be passionate about it. Power follows passion.
   c. Be a faithful steward of *what you do have.*

So the label on God's prescription for worry reads, "In everything by *prayer and supplication, with thanksgiving,* let your requests be made known to God; and the peace of God, which surpasses all understanding, *will guard your hearts and minds* through Christ Jesus" (Philippians 4:6–7 NKJV, emphasis added).

Wow! We don't have to wrestle, capture, or force anything or anyone. We simply pray thankful, believing prayers, and Jesus keeps our hearts and minds at peace. What an amazing solution!

Jesus said, "Peace I leave with you, My peace I give to you; not as the world gives do I give to you. Let not your heart be troubled, neither let it be afraid" (John 14:27 NKJV). When we pray thankful prayers, Christ gives us *His peace* and we are no longer troubled or afraid. So God's antidote for

worry or anxiety is to pray with thanksgiving. Always . . .
today . . . now . . . celebrate!

In the next chapter we'll begin to make the practical
application of what we've learned.

7

SINGLE-MINDED PRAYER

(Part One)

*If any of you lacks wisdom, let him ask of God, who
gives to all liberally and without reproach, and it will be
given to him. But let him ask in faith, with no doubt-
ing, for he who doubts is like a wave of the sea driven
and tossed by the wind.* For let not that man suppose
that he will receive anything from the Lord; *he is a
double-minded man, unstable in all his ways.*

JAMES 1:5–8 NKJV, EMPHASIS ADDED

Would you pray if you thought God wouldn't answer you?
Hardly. If you're like me, you would likely consider it a waste
of time. In this passage James tells us that unless we pray
single-mindedly, we should not expect to receive any answers
to our prayers. But the question is: What is single-minded
prayer? When you pray, are you praying single-mindedly?

Don't be too quick to answer that question until we've looked at this a little more closely.

PRAYER SHOULD BE CONGRUENT

The power of single-minded prayer is all about congruency. Webster defines *congruency* as "a point of agreement." James says if we need wisdom, we should ask God—pray. But when we pray, he says, we must believe, not doubt, and pray in agreement with God's will. The person who doubts when he prays will receive nothing. Why? Because doubt is "double-mindedness," which is contrary to God's nature—it's incongruent!

I recently wrote a check incorrectly. As soon as I noticed my mistake, I wrote "Void" across the face of the check and corrected my register, which of course rendered the check worthless.

When we pray, we write a check on our heavenly account. That check, when written according to God's will, becomes due and payable in heaven. Unfortunately, many of us inadvertently write "Void" on our checks as soon as we leave the prayer room. We believe we're praying in faith, but when put under God's CAT scan, it reveals that we aren't praying single-mindedly at all. Our self-talk (meditation), our conversations, and our behavior regarding our request demonstrate different, even conflicting, expectations. Our prayers are incongruent, or double-minded.

When my friend and motivational speaker Peter Lowe speaks of congruency in life in his Get Motivated seminars, he points out that he'd rather have a Honda Civic with all four wheels pointing in the same direction than the world's most expensive car with wheels pointed in different directions. The Honda isn't the most luxurious car made, but it will get you where you want to go if the wheels are pointed in the same direction. Let's use his example and consider what I call "the four wheels of prayer." Remember, congruency is when all four wheels align.

WHEEL NUMBER ONE: HOW WE MAKE OUR REQUEST

> *Do not be anxious about anything, but in everything, by prayer and petition, with thanksgiving, present your requests to God. And the peace of God, which transcends all understanding, will guard your hearts and your minds in Christ Jesus.*
> PHILIPPIANS 4:6–7

Pray Without Anxiety

Here Paul warns us not to pray anxiety-ridden, worry-filled prayers. Instead, we are to *pray* faith-filled prayers and make our *petitions* (requests of God) with thanksgiving. *Gratitude* and *anxiety* cannot coexist. Either gratitude will displace anxiety, or anxiety will supersede gratitude.

An anxious person is double-minded. He believes in prayer, and believes that God answers prayer, but he's not certain he can trust God to answer *his* prayer.

Prayer with thanksgiving is an expression of our faith. When we step out in faith we defeat unbelief and anxiety. Praise in prayer is the door that allows thanksgiving and faith to meet. Matthew 13:58 tells us that Jesus couldn't do many mighty works in Nazareth because of the people's unbelief (lack of faith).

Pray According to God's Will—His Purposes

It's not enough for us to know God's will, His purposes, and His ways; we must shape our prayers accordingly. Remember, He will answer according to His will.

For example, a wife's anxious (although sincere) prayer for God to save her lost husband might sound like this: *"O Lord, I'm begging you to save my husband. He's such a good man. . . ."* Whoa, hold on! Jesus didn't die on the cross for "good men." He came to seek and to save lost sinners. In this prayer, the wife is suggesting to God that because her husband is decent, even good (in a natural sense), *he deserves* to be saved.

She'll never persuade God to save her husband because He owes it to him. Scripture clearly teaches that God will be a debtor to no one.

You might think the following prayer is better, but is it? *"O Lord, the kids need a saved daddy, and I need a saved husband. Please save him."*

While true enough, this isn't the highest motive from which to pray. It isn't wrong per se; but like the first prayer, she's missing the point. *God saves people for His own glory.* Evangelism isn't as much about *saving people from hell* as it is *saving people for heaven.* It's more about filling the Father's house with children. It's ultimately about the Father's heart.

What about this one? *"God, Mary and Jane have saved husbands. When are you going to save my husband?"*

Perhaps this is the least effective prayer. Why? She is whining to God about her circumstances. The interpretation of this prayer is, "God, it's all about me and what I want." As we've seen, God doesn't "owe" her husband, nor does He "owe" her. That's why we call it "grace."

She wants to see her husband saved. God wants to see him saved too. He's not willing that any should perish. God loves her and her husband. While it's true that God loves us, it is His plan, His purpose, and His glory that move Him to answer our prayers and solve our problems. (See 1 John 5:14.)

Then how should she pray for her lost spouse?

She might pray:

> *Lord, I thank you that Jesus died for my husband's sins. Like me, he deserves nothing from you, Lord. Today I thank you for extending your grace and mercy to him, as you have to me. I thank you that you are saving my husband for your own glory. Establish your kingdom in his heart and glorify your name in his life. Fill him with all that you are, so he can accomplish the purpose for which you have given him life.*

Similar prayers can be prayed for the salvation of a wife, relatives or friends, for wayward children, financial needs, or any other issues you may face. Carefully craft your prayers around the purposes of God and load them with praise and thanksgiving. Like a spiritual attorney, you are pleading your case before Judge Jehovah. Wisely prepare your case before you plead it. This is no time to be running into heaven's courtroom, praying hit-or-miss prayers. God is at work extending His kingdom. Lives are hanging in the balance. For more on this issue, see our book *The Advocates: How to Plead the Cases of Others in Prayer*, available at *www.prayerbookstore.com.*

Too often our prayers are focused on either our problem or our perceived solution to the problem. God wants us to focus on Him! When we focus on Him, our hearts are kept in perfect peace, as promised in Philippians 4:7. Our focus on God is evidence that we are walking by faith and leaving both the problem and the solution to Him.

Renowned pastor Jack Hayford tells how his mother continually prayed one specific prayer for him. It was that God's purposes would be accomplished in his life.

What problem are you facing today? Rather than pray frantic, anxiety-ridden prayers for a solution, why don't you submit your problem to God and His purposes in faith-filled prayer? God wants to do more than simply solve your problem. He wants to demonstrate His miraculous, creative power—*for His own glory*—in the matter. Thank Him in advance for doing so! Praise Him. He inhabits your praise!

Pray With Thanksgiving

There are two reasons it's often hard for us to make our requests with thanksgiving. First, we become so mentally and emotionally focused on our *need*, we wrestle with anxiety. The second reason is that we typically thank someone for doing something *after* they have done it, not before they've begun. When it comes to effective prayer, our thanksgiving (praise) is to both precede *and* follow God's response.

As amazing as it sounds, there was no specific Hebrew word in the Old Testament for "thank-you." To thank someone in ancient Hebrew, you would *bless him* or *praise him* publicly. For example, to thank Omar for giving you a camel, you might say to others, in his presence, "This is my friend Omar. He gave me this fine camel." In the Psalms, God asks us to praise Him in the sanctuary, among the people. From God's perspective, that's gratitude!

When I praise God in advance for doing what I am asking Him to do, I'm praying with expectancy. My thanksgiving is evidence that I am expecting and looking for measurable results from my prayer. When Alice was pregnant with our children, we said, "She is expecting." When I am praying in faith, with the evidence of pre-thanksgiving, I am praying expectantly. Just as a pregnant woman has the expectation of seeing her baby born, I expect to see God answer my prayer in an observable, verifiable way.

My expectant prayer is proof that I believe the following:

- **God alone has the solution to my problem.**

- **I have the right to ask.**

- **God will do what I am asking Him to do (within the bounds of His will).**

There's more here than meets the eye. My praise-filled prayer is more than mere wishful thinking. Yes, indeed. I'm basing my request on God's character (who He is, what He's done in the past, and what He's promised to do in the future). I'm walking by faith, not by sight, and I'm focusing on what I *don't see* rather than on what I *do see*. I'm now praying from an eternal perspective—God's perspective! (See 2 Corinthians 4:18.)

I'm not so much praying for what I want God to do (future tense). I'm praising Him and thanking Him for what He is doing *now*. And how can I be sure that He's doing it now? Because I *know Him*. I understand His promises. I recognize His purposes. And I place my faith in His character. He is doing (right now) what He has promised to do!

As Dr. Charles Blair points out, Christ gives us a business offer that sounds too good to be true, but it's one that we shouldn't refuse. Jesus says, "If you diligently seek me and believe that I am who I say I am and that I do what I've promised I will do, I will reward you." (See Hebrews 11:6.) Wow! What a deal!

Earlier I directed your attention to the contrast between Old and New Testament prayer. My point was to encourage you to pray according to your contract with God (New Testament) rather than pray according to the contract Old Testament saints were limited to. Hebrews 8:13 speaks of the old covenant being made obsolete by the new one. As I pointed out, we have many distinct advantages.

However, that doesn't mean that we can't learn from the prayers recorded in the Old Testament. James points to Elijah as an example to us of a faith-filled prayer warrior. (See James 5:17–18.) David believed so strongly that God was a faithful, promise-keeping God that he often thanked God in advance for what He was about to do! Sometimes celebration is a shout of victory. Sometimes it's a declaration of war.

Do you remember the Passover celebration in Exodus chapter 13? God instructed the children of Israel to celebrate the Passover every year, which they do to this day. But there was a purpose for the celebration. It was to *remember* how God had brought them out of the land of Egypt. There's only one problem, though. . . .

Where was the first Passover celebrated? It was celebrated *in Egypt*. That's right. They were instructed to celebrate their exodus *before* they ever experienced it!

First we pray with thanksgiving, and then God moves. We *celebrate* the answer, then we *see* the answer! As long as we whine to God about our problems, we'll see nothing. Begin to celebrate God's answer, and He will show it to you!

Thanksgiving (praise) precedes the miracle. Let's look at some other biblical examples.

• **Praise preceded the fall of Jericho's walls.**

At God's command the children of Israel marched around the walls of Jericho once each day for six days. On the seventh day they marched around the city seven times, then seven priests blew their ram's horns and the people shouted. (See Joshua 6.) Then, as the old spiritual says, "The walls came a-tumblin' down." Their celebration of trumpets and shouts *preceded* the miracle. After all, anyone could have celebrated *after* the walls fell.

• **Praise preceded Jehoshaphat's victory.**

The prophet Jahaziel told Jehoshaphat and the children of Israel to ignore the threats of the combined armies of the Moabites and Ammonites. He told them it was God's war, not theirs, and that they wouldn't have to lift a finger in battle. They were to stand firm and fearlessly trust God. At Jahaziel's word, Jehoshaphat and all Judah and Jerusalem knelt down and bowed their faces to the ground; the Levites stood to their feet and praised God at the top of their lungs!

The next day Jehoshaphat appointed a choir that marched *ahead of the army,* singing, "Give thanks to the Lord, for his love endures forever" (2 Chronicles 20:21). Their enemies were already in full attack mode, but the moment they began singing, shouting, and praising God, He set angelic ambushes against their enemies. When Israel crested the hill, expecting to see their enemies arrayed in full battle mode, they found them all dead. The Lord had so confused them that they killed one another! Again, celebration preceded the miracle. (See 2 Chronicles 20:14–24 for the full story.)

- **Praise preceded the feeding of the five thousand.**

Jesus had five thousand hungry men and their families to feed with only five barley loaves and two fish. First, He prayed and gave thanks, and then He fed them all—with leftovers to boot! When I heard this as a child, I naturally concluded that Jesus was thanking God for the meal when He prayed. But I was wrong. Jesus wasn't giving thanks for the five loaves and two fish. Why would He do that? It makes no sense. There's no way a lad's lunch could feed more than five thousand people. Jesus was thanking the Father for the miracle that was about to occur. Again, the thanksgiving (celebration) preceded the miracle. (See Mark 6:30–44.)

- **Praise preceded the resurrection of Lazarus.**

Jesus was face-to-face with death. His close friend Lazarus had lain dead in the tomb for three days. Interestingly, Jesus didn't address "death." Instead, He spoke life into the tomb and into Lazarus' body. But look carefully at what He actually did.

> *Then they took away the stone from the place where the dead man was lying. And Jesus lifted up His eyes and said, "Father, I thank You that You have heard Me. And I know that You always hear Me, but because of the people who are standing by I said this, that they may believe that You sent Me." Now when He had said these things, He cried with a loud voice, "Lazarus, come forth!"*
> JOHN 11:41–43 NKJV, EMPHASIS ADDED

Jesus did two things. First, by faith *He thanked the Father in advance* for always hearing Him and for answering His prayer. Only then, after that expression of gratitude, did He call Lazarus out of the tomb.

Jesus prayed in faith, making His request with thanksgiving. "Father," He said, "Thank you for always hearing me." This was no wimpy, secret prayer. He prayed it aloud, where everyone could hear. Then He shouted, "Lazarus, come out!"

When you don't expect God to answer, you don't recognize His answers. When you don't recognize God's answers, you don't celebrate them. When you don't celebrate God's answers, He stops answering! The reason we *see* so little breakthrough is because we *expect* so little. Our lack of expectancy is another of our greatest sins.

- **Praise preceded the earthquake and jailbreak in Philippi.**

Paul and Silas had faithfully preached the gospel in Philippi. For that they were arrested, brutally beaten, and chained in the belly of Philippi's jail. Bloodied, black and blue, when the average person would have assumed that God had failed them, they began to sing, praise, and give thanks to God at midnight. (See Acts 16:20–34.)

The result? An earthquake, a prison break, the salvation of the jailer and his entire family, and a citywide revival! But their miracle was predicated on their midnight praise service where they offered God celebration in advance.

- **Praise preceded the miracle in Brazil.**

A couple of years ago I was teaching in a conference in beautiful Sao Paulo, Brazil. What an amazing city! One of the other international speakers had a great idea. He sent one of his books to Brazil ahead of time to be translated and printed in Portuguese. Upon his arrival in São Paulo, he would pick up his books from the printer, sell them during the conference, and use the money from the sales to pay the printer. Then he would leave the remaining books to be distributed by the pastors. His plan sounded great "on paper." However . . .

When he arrived, the printer told him that the paper on which the books were to be printed had not yet arrived. But no problem—his books would be ready first thing Friday morning. Oops, problem! The conference ended on Thursday night. He wouldn't be able to sell the books at the conference as planned. Plus, he was now faced with a $3,000 printing bill, which he could not pay.

Being a man of integrity, he was heartsick. He came to me on Thursday night clearly distraught. "What am I to do? I must pay the printer tomorrow and pick up the books. I have no money, the conference is over, and I don't need to take the books back home with me. No one in my country speaks Portuguese!"

I said, "It sounds to me like you need a miracle."

"No kidding!" he said, rather helplessly. "What am I to do?"

"We need to *thank God* for solving this problem," I explained.

"But that's just it. God hasn't solved the problem," he protested, still focused on his problem instead of God's promise. What promise? God's promise to do "exceedingly abundantly above all that he could . . . think"!

I said, "Yes, and God won't solve the problem until we thank Him. Remember what I taught? Our thanksgiving should always precede the miracle."

There in the hotel lobby I led him in a simple word of prayer. We thanked God for solving his problem. We praised Him in advance for the miracle that was to come.

The next morning he awakened me with a phone call.

"Eddie," he said breathlessly, "you'll never guess what just happened! A businessman who's been at the conference all week heard me tell my story about the books. He called just now and asked if he could have the books for the price of the printing. He's going to pay the printing bill, take possession of the books, and see that they get distributed here in Brazil!"

- **Praise preceded the miracle for Pastor Johnson's son.**

Pastor Johnson (not his real name) and his wife have a son, Jimmy. A gifted young man, the Lord had given Jimmy's parents wonderful promises concerning his future. The problem was that Jimmy was addicted to drugs. One day he was arrested and jailed, facing two felony drug charges, each punishable by five to ninety-nine years in the state penitentiary.

Jimmy spent one night in the county jail, and God graciously provided a miracle. Partly because he hadn't been in trouble with the law previously, the judge agreed to drop one of the charges, and gave him four years' probation for the other. One night in the county jail was enough to convince Jimmy that he *never* wanted to spend another night there.

However, within the week he got high again and was arrested for violating his probation. His court date was set for approximately thirty days later.

During his month of incarceration Jimmy came to his senses. He realized his need and returned to the Lord.

The night before his trial he called his dad, Pastor Johnson. "Dad, will you be in court for me tomorrow morning?" he asked.

"Son," his dad told him, "your mother and I will both be there. We love you. You and I need to pray right now about tomorrow's trial."

"Dad," Jimmy said, "I don't know how to pray about the trial. I've blown the judge's offer of four years' probation on a five- to ninety-nine-year charge. The only question to be answered tomorrow is *how many* of those ninety-nine years in prison I'll have to serve."

Pastor Johnson said, "Unless . . ."

Jimmy said, "Unless what, Dad?"

"Unless God does what He's promised to do," his dad explained. "He's promised to do 'exceedingly abundantly above all that we can ask' . . . or even think!"

"What do you think God's going to do, Dad?"

"Son, I don't know. It will exceed what either of us can think. Let's praise Him and thank Him now, in advance, for doing that." (Remember: The celebration precedes the miracle.) With that, Pastor Johnson prayed a sincere prayer of thanksgiving for the miracle the Lord was going to perform for Jimmy the next morning.

The next morning Pastor and Mrs. Johnson were sitting in the courtroom. Jimmy was in the holding cell behind a large bolted door. But their family attorney wasn't there, nor was the judge who was to hear the case.

The Johnsons wondered why the trial was delayed. Then their Christian attorney walked in.

He said, "You folks can go home now."

"Go home? Isn't there going to be a trial today?" Pastor Johnson asked.

"It's over," their attorney explained. "I've been practicing law for more than thirty years in this city, and I've never known this to happen before. But Jimmy's judge failed to appear for court. Neither his wife nor his staff know where he is, and he's not answering his cell phone. So your son's case was assigned to another judge—someone who happens to be one of my best friends. He looked through Jimmy's file and asked me, 'What do you want for your client?'"

I told him, "We want ninety days of in-house drug treatment for him, his four-year probation restored, and when it's been served, we want this whole thing expunged from Jimmy's record."

The kind judge said, "You got it." He signed the papers and the case was closed.

That day Jimmy was released to an in-house drug treatment facility, where he was a model client and graduated with honors. A year later he was married to a wonderful Christian girl, and today he serves the Lord in his parents' ministry!

Pastor Johnson also knew that celebration and thanksgiving are to precede the miracle.

Build the Track—the Train Will Follow

There is a world-famous scenic railway over the beautiful snowcapped Alps that stretches from Venice to Vienna. And it has an amazing history. You see, for several years crews laid the track through the icy mountain passes, across the Alpine Mountains, which in itself was thought to be impossible. But stranger still, the track was laid before a train was built that could actually make the trip! When we pray with praise and thanksgiving, as Paul instructs us to do in Philippians 4:6, we are "building a track." At that point, it's God's job to "build the train."

We must offer our thanksgiving in context, however. We cannot pray with thanksgiving when we are not truly thankful. That would be incongruent. We are to be ever mindful of His benefits, not only for the things we want but also for the things we have. "Praise the Lord, O my soul, and forget not all his benefits" says Psalm 103:2. *God never responds to ingratitude.*

The whole idea of celebrating God when we make our requests, or praying with thanksgiving before we see God move, reminds me of the movie *Field of Dreams*. In the movie, Ray Kinsella was inspired to build a baseball field in honor of his deceased father's professional baseball career. His wife, friends, and family thought he was crazy when he told them that while standing in the middle of his profitable cornfield he had heard a voice that said, "If you build it, they will come."

At risk of losing his farm, and people thinking he had lost his mind, Ray built the baseball field in the middle of his cornfield. In the closing scene of the movie, miles of cars are lined up bumper to bumper, making their way to Ray's farm and to the baseball field he had built, to watch famous baseball old-timers play. When we pray with thanksgiving, celebrating in advance what we fully expect God to do, before we've seen any evidence of His response, we are "laying the track," we are "building the ball field." Do it, and watch God respond!

Remember our analogy? It's a car with all four wheels pointed in the same direction. Making our request correctly is the first of the four wheels. In the next chapter we'll look at the other three wheels of prayer that, when in alignment with this first wheel, enable us to pray with congruency and single-mindedness.

8

SINGLE-MINDED PRAYER

(Part Two)

"It is said of Leonardo da Vinci, the great artist, that he would sit practically motionless for days at a time, meditating and getting the inspiration for his masterpieces."[1]

Leonardo understood the importance of meditation. For meditation prepares the heart, clarifies the issues, and focuses on the vision. And vision can produce reality. Before we see how meditation impacts answered prayer, let's summarize.

We are looking at the "four wheels" of single-minded prayer, which must be aligned properly to achieve congruency. Simply put, all four wheels must be pointed in the same direction for us to truly attain single-mindedness in prayer. And what is the point of single-minded prayer? God only answers single-minded prayer. (See James 1:6–8.)

We've looked at the first wheel—*Our Request*. We've learned that our request must be . . .

- made in accordance with God's will;

- prayed in faith, without doubt or worry; and

- accompanied by praise. (We thank God *before,* as well as *after,* He works. We pray with thanksgiving.)

Okay, you've moved from problem-centered to purpose-driven prayer; you're praying in faith, submitting your requests according to God's purposes (the extension of His kingdom and the glory of His name, not simply your need); and you are thanking and praising Him in advance, whether or not there is any visual evidence of His working. But are you single- or double-minded?

Remember, the request is only the first of the "four wheels" that must be aligned (in agreement). If just one of the wheels is pointing in a different direction than the rest, we are incongruent, which has the effect of writing "Void" across our prayer.

WHEEL NUMBER TWO: OUR MEDITATION

Our *request* is how we frame and present our prayer to God. What about our *meditation*? It's not just crazy people who talk to themselves. We all do. Sure you do. The question is, "What are you telling yourself?"

You can "void" a perfectly made prayer request by allowing your thoughts to run *contrary* to it. The psalmist prayed that both the words of his mouth *and* the meditations of his heart would be acceptable to God (see Psalm 19:14). To pray single-minded, productive prayers, our "heart talk" must agree with the words we speak. If we are saying one thing and thinking another, we are double-minded—unstable—as James 1:8 says. So it's important that these first two wheels of our car be pointed in the same direction.

We speak out of the abundance of our hearts (see Matthew 12:34), and we are as we think (see Proverbs 23:7 KJV). The words of our heart can undo the words of our prayer. Have you considered the fact that God "hears" your thoughts as loudly as He hears your words? (See 1 Chronicles 28:9; Psalm 94:11; Psalm 139:23.) To Him, your words and your thoughts are the same.

If you pray for the salvation of a loved one, but continually doubt in your heart that God will save him or her, you are walking by sight, not by faith. For further direction, see Philippians 4:8! Memorize and meditate on this verse.

At this point, you have two of your four wheels aimed in the right direction. Let's look at the third wheel, which is your *conversation*, or *what you say*.

WHEEL NUMBER THREE: OUR CONVERSATION

James points out that fresh and salty water cannot come from the same fountain (see James 3:11). The tongue, he says, is like a tiny rudder that steers a great ship (James 3:4–5). Our tongues are powerful. It's important that *what we say* lines up with *what we pray*.

Try this. Listen to the things you say throughout the course of an average day. You may discover that although you are praying faith-filled prayers in agreement with God's will, and you are expressing gratitude to God in advance, your conversation belies your praying.

Here's an example. Janice needs money for her apartment rent. She prays fervently, believing, thanking God in advance for His provision. So far, so good. Thirty minutes later, however, someone asks about her rent situation. She replies, "I don't know. Things look pretty bleak. I don't know what I am going to do. I'm out of options." In one unguarded conversation, Janice writes "Void" across the prayer she just prayed. Why did she do that?

What she did exposes an underlying issue of unbelief. She prayed the right words, but she wasn't actually praying them in faith. She didn't truly believe them in her heart.

If we could search her heart, as God does, we might discover that Janice is still looking for another option, a source (other than God). By telling another person her need and expressing a level of desperation, she subconsciously hopes that he or she will assist . . . in case God doesn't come through. It's like having a "Plan B." She may not even be aware that she does this, but it's a classic case of being double-minded.

Or perhaps there is an underlying problem with something else she has not yet dealt with—her spending habits. If she's not tithing, or she has wasted what God has given her, she subconsciously knows that God can't bless her. It would be hard for her to really believe, and pray in faith, that God will provide anything for her, knowing in her heart that she has "robbed" Him according to Malachi 3:9–10.

Rather than confess her sin, make restitution, and be restored, she sweeps that under the carpet and expects God to bless her regardless of her past behavior. And it ain't gonna happen! (Pardon the slang.) She needs to have her financial house in order if she expects God to hear and answer her. When God sees that she is trusting Him alone rather than anyone or anything else (no Plan B), He's moved by her faith and honored to answer her.

To honor God, *the words we say* should match *the words we pray*. Our conversations with others should reflect the faith with which we prayed. To pray one thing about a person, place, or circumstance, and then confess the opposite is double-minded; it produces nothing. When someone asks Janice about her rent situation, she would honor God if she answered, "I still don't know how God will do it, but I'm convinced that He is my source and that He's working now to supply all my needs according to His riches in glory, by Christ Jesus" (Philippians 4:19 NKJV). "And for that, I give Him praise."

WHEEL NUMBER FOUR: OUR BEHAVIOR

Three of the four wheels are pointed in the same direction. They are congruent. But there's one other wheel that must be brought into alignment with them if we are to make progress in prayer. There's one more way we can even unintentionally "void" our prayer. Or, to put a positive spin on it, we have one more opportunity to express our faith when we pray. *Our behavior* is also an outward expression of an inward attitude. If we behave in a manner that is inconsistent with our request, our meditation, and our conversation, we are double-minded. The following example should be helpful in illustrating this principle.

Mary has prayed for her husband, Ben, for twenty-four years. Ben has no time for God and shows virtually no interest in coming to know Him. The problem is that although Mary prays faithfully for Ben's salvation, she treats him like her "spiritual junior."

When they were first married, he was "the man of her dreams." But she has elevated herself and her relationship with God above him now, and believe me, he feels it. She'd never believe how hurtful this can be to a man who knows almost nothing about Christ. For a man to share his wife's affection with another man is difficult. But how does one compete for the affection of his wife with a man he cannot see?! Trust Christ? Love God? How can he do that? Christ (in his mind) has come between him and his wife.

Actually, I know of many examples of wives of lost husbands whose relationship with Christ has made them so adoring of and affectionate toward their husbands that their husbands are actually grateful for their wives' commitment to Christ. In Mary's case, she must begin to treat Ben like the man she *wants him to be,* instead of the man *he currently is,* if she's going to convince Ben, God, and others that she already sees him (with the eyes of faith) saved! When she begins to show Ben the respect and honor due a spiritual man, God will move according to her expectation. Now that's faith in action.

Belief in Action

Before Alice's brother John knew the Lord, she prayed faithfully for his salvation. When we visited him we avoided any references to the ministry because we knew that he wouldn't relate well to them. Then one day the Lord gave Alice a word that He was going to save John. He even told her the city in which he would be saved. And He led us to do something quite unusual. The Lord told us to treat John not as he was, but as though he were *already* saved. After all, that was what we were trusting God for!

So the next time we were with John, we talked openly about the people that had recently been born again in our meetings and the wonderful things God was doing in our ministry. We applied it directly to him, saying, "John, you would have loved it."

Months later, after John came to Christ, he told us, "You guys don't know this, I'm sure. But one of the things that caused me to come to Christ was a change in the way you treated me. Always before, you treated me as though we had nothing in common. But about six months ago you began treating me like I was 'one of you.' The more you treated me like I was a believer, the more I realized I wasn't, and the more I wished I were."

James Stewart (not the American actor) was a Welshman who was greatly used of God in the nineteenth century Welsh revival. His mother was a powerful praying woman. In his youth, James hadn't yet trusted Christ as his Savior. As you can imagine, this greatly concerned his godly mother.

One day his mother came to James and said, "Son, I've spoken with our youth pastor at the church, and he is making room in the next month's youth service for you to share your salvation testimony."

"Salvation testimony?" he gulped. "What are you talking about? I don't have a salvation testimony, Momma. I'm going to hell and play football" (his word for soccer).

Undaunted by his insolence, she continued praying and believing God. Every other day or so she would remind him, "Son, don't forget your next month's youth service.

We're counting on you to give your salvation testimony for Christ."

He would blurt back his now typical response, "Momma, I've told you, I'm going to hell and play football."

One day he passed a lady on the street, who smiled and said, "James, I hear you're giving your salvation testimony at the next youth service." He said, "That's just my crazy mother. I'm going to hell and play football."

One day at soccer practice James was running across the field when something unusual happened—he tripped, slipped, or perhaps was pushed to the ground by the Holy Spirit. All he remembered was that with his face in the sod, he met God. In a mere moment, his life was instantly and eternally changed!

James jumped up. Without explanation to anyone, he ran off the field and down the street to his home. Up the sidewalk he darted, across the porch, and through the house toward the kitchen, all the while screaming, "Momma, Momma, I got saved, I got saved, Momma!"

With hardly any expression of surprise, she looked up from her dishes and calmly said with a smile, "Why son, I've been trying to tell you that for the past month."

James' mother was no worrier—she was a warrior. She was not a whiner—she was a winner. She was committed to God's purposes, believed God's promises, and put her faith in His power to keep them. She prayed congruent, single-minded prayers!

where's the PRAISE *party?*

MY FRIEND ZIG Ziglar is such an optimist, he says that he would go after Moby Dick in a rowboat and take the tartar sauce with him! Knowing Zig . . . I believe him! As I write this book, Zig, a wonderful Christian statesman and internationally famous motivational speaker in his eighties, still speaks in more than fifty events per year! He definitely knows how to celebrate life, and this is an important key to answered prayer. Remember what I said earlier: *God never responds to ingratitude.* No matter how bad things get, if you are a grateful person, you can find something to be grateful for. Focus on that, and you'll find more. However, if you focus on your disadvantages and discomfort, you'll find more of them as well! Whatever you focus on expands.

Once we have "made our case" to God in prayer, we are to begin the process of watching—to *watch and pray,* as Jesus put it. In Colossians 4:2, Paul says: "Devote yourselves to prayer, being watchful and thankful." What are we to look for? We're looking for even the slightest indication of God's response. Why? So we can throw a praise party, of course. Worriers and whiners throw "pity parties." Zig warns, "The problem with pity parties is, nobody shows up!" Warriors and winners throw "praise parties!" When you throw a "praise party," God always shows up.

Suppose a woman is praying for her lost husband, and one day he turns (uncharacteristically) to her and says, "Pray for Jim's wife. She is going in for some cancer tests today." Whoa! Here is a lost man who's making *a prayer request*! It's time for his wife to throw a party!

What about the mother who's praying for her wayward son at 3:00 a.m.? She's lying facedown on the living room carpet crying out to the Lord, when he staggers drunkenly through the front door toward his room. He reflexively says, "Prayer woman, you can go to bed. I'm home." Then as he gets to the door of his bedroom, he looks over his shoulder and says, "And you can pray for Tommy's mother. They say she has cancer and needs surgery." As he slams his bedroom door behind him, she cries out, "O Lord, when are you going to do something with my boy?"

Whoa! She really missed it. Let's take a closer look.

1. Other drunken sons died or were dismembered in head-on collisions tonight. Some were arrested and are spending the night in jail. Her son came home safely.
2. Look at what he called his mother: "prayer woman." He knows who she is. He recognizes her kingdom role.
3. Besides that, he gave her a prayer request! Deep inside, he knows she has access to a power greater than his.

It's time for her to call some friends and throw a praise party. Well, perhaps not. After all, it's three in the morning! But it's certainly time for her to begin to see and celebrate God's work in her son's life. Subtle? Sure, it's subtle. God's work is often subtle. That's our test. Are we focused on the demonstrations of their flesh and the devil in their lives? Or are we focusing on evidences of God's work? As we learn to focus on what He is doing rather than on these negative demonstrations or what we want (our plans), we'll see it.

Begin to listen carefully to the things the people you are praying for say, and things they do, in their unguarded moments. These are often unconscious expressions of what's going on inside them. When you see anything, the slightest thing, that is positive, record it. That's right, write it down—journal it. And begin to praise God for it. Perhaps you have a child who is often angry, rebellious, and disrespectful. When you see him do something, any kind or respectful thing toward anyone, celebrate it. Thank God for it! As you acknowledge God, the frequency and size of His activity will increase. He loves your celebration. It's the atmosphere of heaven!

To use a sports analogy, anyone can celebrate the final score, but God wants us to celebrate *every point* that goes on the board! Every point that appears on the board is additional evidence that God is at work . . . and that warrants our praise! Rather than waiting expectantly, identifying and celebrating what the Father is doing in answer to our prayer, too many of us have already turned our attention back to another "need" we plan to present to Him. Don't you imagine He's tired of being ignored?

King David said, "My voice You shall hear in the morning, O Lord; in the morning I will direct it [my prayer] to

You, *And I will look up*" (Psalm 5:3 NKJV). The Contemporary English Version says, *"wait for your reply."* After directing his prayer to God, David would watch and wait expectantly for an answer.

Ask God with thanksgiving, then watch expectantly for any evidence of His divine intervention in the matter, no matter how small it is. While it's true that I pray based on *who God is* and *what He's said and done* in the past, I do expect to see expressions of His intervention. As I pray, I carefully watch for evidences of His answers to my prayers. As I said, it's a good idea to journal these answers. Reading back over them later will build your faith for future prayer projects.

Be prepared for this: God often moves in slight, subtle, incremental ways. It is especially difficult for us who live in an "instant culture" to relate to an eternal God for whom one day is as a thousand years. Impatient and with short attention spans, we want instant gratification—and we want it *now*! When we don't immediately get what we've asked for, we lose faith.

Why does God move so slowly and with such small steps? Possibly because . . .

1. He is testing your faith.
2. He's checking to see if you are paying attention to Him.
3. He wants to know if you will celebrate even His smallest response.
4. He wants to extend your celebration over a longer period of time.
5. He's working behind the scenes to prepare people, places, and things (including you) for what He's about to do. All this takes time.

Could it be that we "void" our prayers by failing to celebrate the small stuff? It's easy for us to be so enamored with the splitting of the Red Sea that we neither notice nor appreciate God's incremental answers to our prayers, as when He made the wheels of Pharaoh's chariots fall off!

Perhaps you, like me, tend to become frustrated. Your inclination is to "fold up your prayer tent and go home" when you don't see some great answer to your prayer. Well, it's time that we begin to notice the tiny adjustments and expressions of God's intervention. Watch so carefully that when you see the slightest thing, celebrate it! Throw a praise party!

Worse still, many times when we see God's reponse to our prayer (His blessing), we either express our lack of faith with statements like, "You wouldn't believe what God did"; "It's unbelievable"; etc., or we actually take credit with statements like, "It's the result of my clean living." And perhaps most often, we respond with, "Wow! What a coincidence!" It's no coincidence. It's a "God-incidence!"

In the Old Testament temple, there were priests whose duty it was to watch for the manifest presence of the Shekinah glory of the Lord. God is calling us, as His New Testament priests, to intentionally identify, acknowledge, and celebrate even His smallest response. Give Him glory!

Ingratitude grieves God as much as unbelief does. If you ignore the small things God does in answer to your prayer, you'll not see much. So take note: Consider right now something the Lord has done for you. Now deliberately praise Him for it! Go ahead, I'll wait. You will begin to experience a bubbling up in your soul. That joy will explode into a smile on your face and a spring in your step. Amazingly, your disappointment and frustrations are fading, aren't they?

Elijah knew this thrill. After ordering the killing of 850 prophets of Baal and Asherah, he ascended to the top of Mount Carmel to pray for rain. But what he saw next was most unusual. It wasn't rain. It wasn't even a rain cloud. There was no thunder or lightning; there was only a cloud "as small as a man's hand" (1 Kings 18:44). Elijah saw a "micro cloud" and turned to Ahab and said, "You'd better get off of this mountain. There's a serious storm coming." As he rejoiced to see God at work, that small cloud grew into a mighty rainstorm that ended a three-year-long drought!

My granddaddy Jeff had a large pickle jar full of coins that sat on the floor of his closet. I know now that it was the place he threw his pocket change. My two younger brothers and I spent each summer at our grandparents' home near Gadsden, Alabama. We looked forward to the times when we were allowed to stick our arm into granddaddy's coin jar. We could keep everything we could grasp in one hand!

As children, we thought that the coin jar experience was for us. However, now that I'm a granddaddy myself, I realize that it was just as much (if not more) for my grandparents' pleasure. They looked forward to those days with as much excitement as we did. They loved to see the looks of celebration on our faces, as I do when my grandchildren reach into my coin jar.

What about the coins? When we were young, we could never grasp much more than a dollar's worth, yet we were thrilled. We looked forward with anticipation to the next year, when our hands would grow larger. Is it possible we older Christians have grown so calloused that we overlook the small things our heavenly Daddy does in answer to our prayer? Walter Knight has said, "Joy is the flag that flies over the castle of our hearts announcing that the King is in residence."[1] Does the "joy flag" fly above your life today, announcing the King's presence?

CELEBRATE THE SMALL STUFF!

We are to celebrate God's smallest responses to our prayers. The psalmist David said, "I will praise God's name in song and glorify him with thanksgiving" (Psalm 69:30). The verse that follows says, "This will please the Lord more than [my sacrificing] an ox, more than a bull with its horns and hoofs." Jesus said in John 14:13, "I will do whatever you ask in my name, so that the Son may bring glory to the Father." Interesting, isn't it? Answering our prayer is one of the ways that Jesus glorifies the Father.

In Exodus 15, after crossing the Red Sea and escaping the wrath of Pharaoh and his army, the children of Israel threw a praise party to celebrate God for bringing them safely out of Egypt. Do you see it? They had praised God by faith (the Passover celebration) *before* they experienced their exodus. Here they praised God *after* they experienced their exodus.

Are you so aware of God's blessings in your life that you *can* declare them? Are you so grateful for God's blessings in your life that you *do* declare them?

In the mid to late 1800s, George Mueller ran an orphanage and was responsible for the care and feeding of thousands of orphaned children. He never asked anyone for their financial support. He chose to rely upon God. Because of God's response to George Mueller's prayer, he became known as "the apostle of answered prayer."

At the age of ninety, Mr. Mueller was interviewed about his journal of answered prayer. The journalist asked him, "Mr. Mueller, have you ever had a prayer not answered?" Indignantly and instantly Mueller declared, "Never. However," he said, "I have been praying fifty-two and one-half years for the salvation of a son of a friend. He isn't saved yet, but he will be."

Was that the ranting of an arrogant old man? Hardly. His friend's son was born again at Mueller's own funeral, as Mueller's body was being lowered into the grave!

Before this, no one had ever known how many answered prayers Mueller had experienced. After his death, at age ninety-three, Mueller's journal was opened, and his recorded answers to prayer were counted. He had documented more than fifty thousand answers to prayer!

Mueller, like King David, had decided to bless the Lord and *never forget* His benefits (see Psalm 103:2).

What about you? If you were to die, what would they find recorded in your journal? Would they find fifty thousand *answers* to prayer, or fifty thousand prayer *requests*?

MAGNIFY THE LORD

In Luke 1:46, Mary begins her song of praise by saying, "My soul magnifies the Lord" (NKJV). Since childhood that has puzzled me. "Magnify" the Lord? He's omnipresent. How do you magnify someone who's *as big as He can be*?

I presented my dilemma to our board of directors one day. Glenn, who is much smarter than me, explained that when we magnify the Lord we don't make Him bigger at all. He asked me if I'd ever owned a magnifying glass as a child. I assured him that in elementary school I had owned an official Cub-Scout-issue magnifying glass, with which I had incinerated millions of ants.

Pressing past my lame attempts at humor, he explained, "Eddie, when you magnified an insect with your magnifying glass, you didn't make the insect bigger; you *saw* it bigger." I got it! I saw the insect bigger—that's it. So to magnify the

Lord is to see and celebrate God's blessings greater than most people would!

How did Mary magnify the Lord? For the next nine verses in Luke 1, she rehearsed aloud the things God had done through the centuries from Abraham to her present day.

The Pharisees wanted Jesus to rebuke the disciples for magnifying Him one day. He said, "I tell you that, if these should hold their peace, the stones would immediately cry out" (Luke 19:40 KJV). Surprisingly, Ezekiel tells us that God *magnifies himself*! "I will show my greatness and my holiness, and I will make myself known in the sight of many nations. Then they will know that I am the Lord" (Ezekiel 38:23).

God Wants the Firstfruits of Our Praise

One day, I was joyfully proclaiming to a friend a miraculous answer to prayer for my family, when God spoke so sweetly to me. He said, "Eddie, I love to hear you celebrate what I've done for you. But when will you begin to offer me the *firstfruits* of your celebration?"

"What do you mean, Lord?" I asked.

He explained, "Well, you know how wonderful you feel when you hear Alice across a crowded room telling someone something she admires about you?"

"Yes," I replied.

"But you know how much *more* rewarding it is when she comes to you in private and tells *you* what she feels about you?"

Sure, I knew the difference.

He said, "That's what I want. I want the firstfruits of your celebration—just me and you. Afterward, you can share it with others."

THE BACKLASH—HOW SATAN ROBS GOD

Satan is no match for God. Because of that, many times Satan won't compete with God for your miracle. Instead, he competes with God for your *response* to the miracle! Don't be surprised if your miracle is followed by a disappointment. Experienced intercessors call that "the backlash." Their general thought is that the devil is trying to get even with them because of their spiritual success. But the truth is, it isn't about them.

Typically, after God has done something wonderful that we are celebrating, the enemy throws discouragement in our path. Why? To distract us from giving God the celebration that He deserves.

The battle is for God's glory, not for our miracle.

If we allow our disappointment to displace our praise, Satan robs God of receiving glory—the reason God did the miraculous to begin with! Face it. Satan is the ultimate "party crasher."

Will we surrender God's celebration to Satan's distraction, or ignore Satan's intrusion on our "praise party" and celebrate God appropriately? What are we most fearful of: that we won't receive our miracle, or that God won't receive His praise?

Alice and I had finished teaching at the convention center in Charlotte, North Carolina, and were headed toward the airport, when we began to witness to the cab driver, who was from Ghana. After a few minutes he prayed to receive Christ as his Lord and Savior. It was glorious!

His tears of joy made it difficult for him to see the road to the airport. When we stopped, he jumped out, hugged us, and thanked us for sharing Christ's life with him. As you can imagine, we didn't need a plane to get home; we could have floated home on "wings of joy."

At the ticket counter Alice was given her boarding pass. Then the woman looked at me and said, "Sir, I'm sorry, but your ticket has been cancelled. You don't have a seat on this flight."

"I didn't cancel my ticket," I told her.

"No. You're right. It appears that the airline cancelled your ticket."

"Well, ma'am, you *are* the airline. Why don't you 'un-cancel' my ticket for me?"

"Sir, I can't do that," she said. "Apparently this issue is between your travel agent and the airline. You'll have to buy another $471 ticket if you plan to fly home on this flight with your wife."

I was fuming inside as I pulled out my credit card and purchased another $471 ticket. I picked up my briefcase and started moping off to the departure gate when God said, "Eddie, why did you sell my praise for $471?" All it took was that one setback, one disappointment, to shut down my "praise party" for the salvation of our cab driver. I had allowed Satan to crash my party and rob God of the praise He was due—for a measly $471. Never again. From now on, I intend to party, backlash or no backlash, just as Paul and Silas partied their way through their backlash in that Philippian prison!

Let me offer one more illustration that will help to make my point. It's fanciful, not grounded in fact, but it does make you think.

A man died and was given a guided tour of heaven. In the first room he saw rows and rows of angels with headsets, seated at desks, frantically writing things down. He asked Saint Peter, his guide, "Who are these angels and what are they doing? Saint Peter explained that they were receiving prayer requests. Then they moved into the next room.

This room, too, was huge and quite busy. Angels were frantically labeling large boxes and placing them on a conveyor belt. "And this room?" the man asked. Saint Peter explained that these angels were answering people's prayers. Then they moved to the third and final room.

This large room was also staffed with angels with headsets. But they seemed to be on a coffee break. They looked bored; they were casually seated, adjusting their wings. The man couldn't help but notice how different this room was from the others. "What is this room for?" he asked his guide.

"This room?" Saint Peter responded, "Oh, this room is our *acknowledgement* room. These angels are responsible for receiving acknowledgement, thanksgiving, and celebration from those whom God has blessed."

God told me one day, "Eddie, if you will celebrate the movement of my finger, I'll move my hand for you. If you will celebrate the movement of my hand, I'll move my arm for you. If you will celebrate the movement of my arm, I'll *move mountains for you*!" Today, heaven is waiting for us to join them in extraordinary celebration. So let's acknowledge, thank, and celebrate every victory that God sends our way. Let's light up heaven's switchboard with magnificent praise, for this is a key to our being heard in heaven!

POSTSCRIPT

Seven Keys in Christ's "Model" Prayer

HAVE YOU EVER mailed a package only to have it returned to you? I'm afraid that a lot of my prayers through the years have been returned "undeliverable." I'm no longer interested in rituals, religion, rote, and routine. I do not want to waste words, insult God, or play games. I want to know how to pray effectively.

Jesus' disciples were no different. One day they asked Him to teach them to pray. I'm convinced that their request wasn't so much "teach us *how to* pray" as it was "teach us how to pray *like you pray*." The disciples knew how to pray. After all, they saw people gather several times a day to pray at the temple during the time of the burning of incense. Theirs was a praying culture. Pharisees were known to pray in the streets. No, they didn't want to simply know how to pray, but how to pray as Jesus prayed. When Jesus prayed, God heard Him and things happened! That was what they wanted to learn. As Christ's disciples today, we want to know the same thing.

Jesus began His instruction on prayer with a strange statement. He said in Matthew 6:32, "The Father knows what you need before you even ask Him" (my paraphrase). Which begs the question: "Well, if He already knows what I need, then what's the point in my asking?" Clearly, based on what Jesus said, its primary purpose is *not* to have our needs met. Jesus went on to say in verse 33 of that same chapter that if we would seek His kingdom first and foremost, our needs would be met. We have been discovering throughout this book what the primary purpose of prayer is: to acknowledge and adore God, to extend His kingdom, and to see the knowledge of His glory cover the earth as the waters cover the sea. (See Habakkuk 2:14.) God's kingdom is His "thing." As we begin to seek "His thing," He'll take care of "our things."

When the disciples asked Jesus to teach them to pray, He responded by giving them a model prayer in which we can find seven keys to effective prayer. In some ways, these keys underscore what we've been learning. Remember, we aren't after some illusive promise that God will answer every prayer or give us all we want. Frankly, if God had given me all I've asked Him for through the years, my life would be a mess today! We're talking about moving up to new levels of maturity in prayer and praying kingdom-oriented prayers, prayers that honor God and accomplish His purposes.

KEYS TO BEING HEARD IN HEAVEN

KEY #1: When you pray to the Father, call Him Daddy. He loves that.

Jesus' model prayer in Matthew 6:9–13 begins with the words: "Our Father in heaven." Interestingly, Jesus' discourse about prayer doesn't begin with man, or man's need. It begins with God. Before He created the earth, God was a Father who had a Son. As mentioned in chapter 2, Old Testament saints could only pray to "the God of Abraham, Isaac, and Jacob." But Jesus prayed to "Abba" (Daddy). And when Jesus prayed, things happened!

Thirteen times the Old Testament refers to God as "Father." (See Deuteronomy 32:6; 2 Samuel 7:14; 1 Chronicles 17:13; 22:10; 28:6; Psalm 68:5; 89:26; Isaiah 9:6; 63:16; 64:8; Jeremiah 31:9; and Malachi 2:10.) However, in the New Testament, Jesus referred to God as *His Father* more than 150 times, and thirty times He refers to God as *our Father*. "Father" is one of God's favorite titles. In the Old Testament He was seen primarily as the Father of the nation, while in the New Testament we see Him as our personal heavenly Father.

When I pray about a personal concern, I have the assurance that Christ is praying *with me* (Hebrews 7:25) and that the Holy Spirit is praying *through me* (Romans 8:26). Ecclesiastes 4:12 tells us that "a cord of three strands is not quickly broken." There is strength when Christ, the Holy Spirit, and you pray in one accord.

John 5:17–18 makes it clear why Jesus' calling God His Father so exasperated the scribes and the Pharisees (Israel's religious leaders). It says,

> Jesus said to them, "My Father is always at his work to this very day, and I, too, am working." For this reason the Jews tried all the harder to kill him; not only was he breaking the Sabbath, but he was even calling God his own Father, making himself equal with God.

Today, we so readily speak of God as our Father that we may have lost the significance of this privilege. It's not until we hear variations of it that it grabs our attention and touches our hearts. I remember hearing an intercessor in Cincinnati, Ohio, as she passionately prayed to her "heavenly Daddy," and "Daddy God." Hearing her call Him that reminded me again of our amazing privilege to know God as Father.

Our second oldest grandson, Adriel, was only about two years old when visiting our house one day. His dad, our son-in-law Baruch (an Israeli), had gone to get something from the car when Adriel came through the room looking for him, crying, "Abba! Abba! Abba!" Abba is the tender title a small Israeli child uses to call his father.

In the model prayer, Jesus invites us to approach God exactly the way He did—as our daddy, our "Abba." Later the apostle Paul wrote in Galatians 4:6, "God sent the Spirit of his Son into our hearts, the Spirit who calls out, 'Abba, Father'." And in Romans 8:15 he wrote, "You received the Spirit of sonship. And by him we cry, 'Abba, Father'."

Since the Holy Spirit is the Spirit of Christ, and Christ referred to God as His Abba, it's no surprise that when our prayer is Spirit-produced and empowered, so will we.

KEY #2: When you pray, brag on His name. He's crazy about His name.

Praise is as indispensable to prayer as fuel is to an automobile. So Jesus tells us to say something like "Hallowed be Your name." (In other words, "Lord, make your name holy.") Even while delivering the children of Israel from Egyptian bondage, God expressed His primary purpose. In Exodus 14 we find them on the shore of the Red Sea with Pharaoh and his army breathing down their necks. They cried out in desperation for God to save them. And three times He said something like "I will get glory from Pharaoh and his army, then everyone will realize that I am God!" Whatever your concern may be in prayer, suggest to God that He make His name holy in the matter! In the final analysis, He does what He does *for His glory*!

KEY #3: When you pray, remind Him that He's the boss.

Say something like, "Your kingdom come, Your will be done on earth as it is in heaven." I once asked my preacher daddy, "Dad, where is the kingdom of God?" He thought for a moment, looked over the top of his glasses with a smile, and said, "Why son, the kingdom of God is anywhere that God is King!"

His kingdom is established in us, and as we grow in knowledge and grace, His kingdom is extended through us! You see, God's never had a boss. He has always been in charge. He answers to no one else. So let Him know that you like it like that.

At this point, you have His complete attention. Now you can begin to present your petitions.

KEY #4: Ask Him to give you your daily bread— what you need for that day.

Rather than give us a once-for-all miraculous provision that would enable us to be independent of Him from that point on, He instructs us to ask for "daily bread" to teach us the discipline of walking by faith. (See Galatians 3:11.)

So we are to ask every day, if we are to receive. We are to continually "lean on His everlasting arms." As we continually place our faith in our Provider, every day's provision is miraculous! Just as the children of Israel were sustained by manna from heaven during their wilderness wandering, God will sustain us. But their supply was daily. And they couldn't eat tomorrow what God provided today. They had to trust Him a day at a time (see Exodus 16:19–21). The psalmist, in Psalm 37:25, said, "I have never seen the righteous forsaken or their children begging bread." Thank God for His faithfulness to feed you and meet your other needs as well.

I believe "bread" in this passage represents all of our material and physical needs. And the significant point here is that we are to ask for them daily . . . every day.

KEY #5: Ask Him to forgive you, as you forgive those who sin against you.

I deal with this at length in my book *Breaking the Enemy's Grip*, published in 2006 by Bethany House Publishers. There is so much to say about the importance of forgiveness that I dedicated two chapters to it. Unforgiveness is poisonous. It does more damage to the vessel in which it is stored than to the person on which it is poured.

In Matthew 5:23–24, Jesus tells us that before we come before God, we must first be reconciled to others. How can we say we love God, whom we cannot see, when we do not love others, whom we can see? I don't forgive others because it's an obligation. My forgiving them is not an admission that what they did wasn't hurtful. I forgive them because Christ died for their sins. I cannot hold them accountable to me when Christ has already paid the price of their sin. To do so would dishonor His sacrifice.

KEY #6: Ask Him for a restraining order against the enemy.

Most of us pray reactive prayers. We wait until the devil assaults us on some level, then we begin to pray against it. It's time for us to learn to pray proactively. Ask God, in advance (proactively), to deliver you from temptation and to place a *restraining order* against the devil on your behalf. God's the Judge! He can do that. The angels of God, which are sent to minister to those of us who are heirs of salvation (see Hebrews 1:14), are heaven's police force. They enforce that law by wrestling with and containing forces of darkness.

James tells us, "When tempted, no one should say, 'God is tempting me.' For God cannot be tempted by evil, nor does he tempt anyone" (James 1:13). So when Jesus instructs us to pray, "Lead us not into temptation," it can be confusing. God doesn't actually *lead* us into temptation. Satan is the source of temptation. Matthew 4:3 and 1 Thessalonians 3:5 speak of him as the tempter. We discover him first as a liar and tempter in the garden of Eden, where he tempted Eve to eat of the forbidden fruit.

Although Satan is the source of temptation, the *instrument* of temptation is our Adamic nature. James writes, "But each one [of us] is tempted when, by his own evil desire, he is dragged away and enticed" (James 1:14). So Satan tempts us now through our lower (sinful) Adamic nature.

If God never leads anyone into temptation, then why would Jesus tell us to ask God not to lead us into temptation?

And why pray for God's protection since Psalm 91 promises us His protection? Interestingly, God feeds and protects the birds without their asking. And He also promises to provide for and protect us.

Unlike the birds, we have an advanced God-given ability to reason, to choose, and to believe. So we are given an additional requirement beyond them. We need to *ask in faith*. James wrote, "You don't have what you want because you don't ask God for it" (James 4:2 NLT).

Sure God has promised to feed us, as He does the birds, but we should still ask Him for our daily bread. He has promised to protect us from temptation and destruction, but we are to ask Him not to lead us into temptation—or allow us to be tempted—and to deliver us from the evil one. Daily we are to pray and ask God for provision, protection, and a heavenly restraining order against the evil one, for ourselves and for our families.

The bottom line is this: God's your Dad. *As long as you are delighting in Him*, you can ask Him for literally anything your heart desires. What you receive will, of course, depend upon His will for you. But go ahead and ask! If you're off target, He'll tell you.

KEY #7: Exit properly.

When leaving the throne room, Jesus said to say something like . . . "For yours is the kingdom and the power and the glory forever. Amen."[1] Let Father God know that your primary concern is the same as His. All you pray is for His kingdom, His power, and His glory.

This model prayer, or as some call it, "The Lord's Prayer,"

along with Christ's prayer life, provide a template or example for us. From His teaching and example we see the qualities that should be evident in our praying. However, we can make a subtle but serious mistake at this point.

A pastor once overheard a woman in his congregation refer to him as "a model pastor." He was unsure what she meant by that. So when he returned to his office he looked up the word *model* in the dictionary. The definition given was: "a cheap imitation of the real thing."

The Christian life isn't about our *imitating* Jesus. That would be a "cheap imitation of the real thing." We're not to imitate Him; we are to allow Him to live His life in and through us—and that includes His prayer life. He didn't come to *repair us*; He came to *replace us*. He is alive, and He's here! It's His life in us, being lived through us, that produces God's glory (see Colossians 1:27). We are to be crucified (executed), and He is to be our life (see Galatians 2:20 and Colossians 3:4).

When He is Lord of our lives, certain qualities of His life, including His prayer life, will inevitably be displayed through us. Death to self and to sin is not the end—it is the means to the end. The end is that Christ's resurrected life can be seen in us for the Father's glory.

Learning about Christ's prayer life isn't for the purpose of *learning to pray* in some formula way. It's so we can learn to recognize when we are praying "in the Spirit." When we are filled with the Holy Spirit (which is the Spirit of Christ), He will pray through us as He did in Galilee two thousand years ago. Why would I think that He would pray differently now than He did then?

One who claims to be a Christian who isn't demonstrating Christ's life, including His prayer life, is deceived. The New

Testament reveals to us the prayer life of Christ as a gauge by which we can measure Christ's activity in us.

So if it's all about Christ and His kingdom, do we still have the right to make our desires known? Can we pray for a specific job that we want, for instance? Absolutely. The psalmist said, "Delight yourself also in the Lord, and He will give you the desires and secret petitions of your heart" (Psalm 37:4 AMP).

And Christ? He demonstrated in the garden of Gethsemane prior to His crucifixion that we can certainly *ask for our desires*. He desired that God would "take this cup" from Him. (See Luke 22:42.) What was the cup? Was it His crucifixion? More than likely it was that awful moment when He would become sin for us, and for the first time God the Father would turn His head away from His Son. Christ had never known the filth of sin, and He didn't want to "become sin" for us. He knew the Father couldn't look upon sin, and He didn't want to be forsaken by the Father. That was His *desire*. Yet the Father didn't allow Jesus to have what He desired on this occasion. Why? Because it wasn't in line with the Father's will. Notice that although Jesus felt perfectly free to express His will to the Father, He never elevated His desire above the Father's will.

Feel free to express your desires to Him. He's your Father, so ask Him for anything you want. But ask with the humility and submission with which Christ asked. Never elevate your desire above His will. He is a God of purpose, and He will only answer our prayers according to His purposes. When you don't know what they are, ask Him to reveal them to you. Then allow Him to sort out the issues as they relate to His will, as Jesus did—"Yet not my will, but yours be done" (Luke 22:42).

Certainly, as any loving father does, God wants us to come to Him with our needs and desires. But don't forget: He is more than our Father. He is the eternal Sovereign Ruler of the universe—a King with a kingdom. As long as our praying extends no further than ourselves, our needs, and our desires, we will never become the kingdom partners God intends for us to be, and we will not see God's kingdom come. Why? Because His kingdom will have to be established *in us* before it can be extended *through us*. (See Luke 17:21.)

There is a difference between what we hear and what we listen to. As you read this line of type you actually *hear* the ambient noises around you. There now . . . now you are *listening* to them. Again, there is a difference between what we *hear* and what we *listen* to, what captures our attention, and in some cases, demands a response from us. I don't want to be a person whom God simply *hears*. I want to be a person to whom He *listens*. I want my prayers to capture His attention. I want Him to lean in to hear what is on my heart. Are you ready to be heard in heaven?

ENDNOTES

Chapter 2

1. Charles Swindoll, *The Tale of the Tardy Oxcart* (Nashville, TN: Word Publishing, 1998), 53.
2. Paul E. Holdcraft, *Cyclopedia of Bible Illustrations* (New York/Nashville: Abingdon-Cokesbury Press, 1947), 122.
3. Larry Libby, "Prayers From the Edge," *Discipleship Journal* (May/June 2006): n.p.

Chapter 3

1. Paul E. Holdcraft, *Cyclopedia of Bible Illustrations* (New York/Nashville: Abingdon-Cokesbury Press, 1947), 232.
2. Charles Swindoll, *The Tale of the Tardy Oxcart* (Nashville, TN: Word Publishing, 1998), 453–54.
3. "Clichés and One-Liners," *worldofquotes.com*.
4. Wesley L. Duewel, *Touch the World Through Prayer* (Grand Rapids: Zondervan, 1986), n.p.
5. Eddie and Alice Smith, *Intercessors* (Houston: SpiriTruth Publishing, 2000), 23–24.

Chapter 5

1. Eddie and Alice Smith, *The Advocates: How to Plead the Cases of Others in Prayer* (Lake Mary, FL: Charisma House Publishing, 2001), 177–78.

Chapter 6

1. Charles Swindoll, *The Tale of the Tardy Oxcart* (Nashville, TN: Word Publishing, 1998), 625.
2. Bill Gothard, quoted in a conference I attended in 1978, Dallas, Texas.

Chapter 8

1. Paul E. Holdcraft, *Cyclopedia of Bible Illustrations* (New York/Nashville: Abingdon-Cokesbury Press, 1947), 182.

Chapter 9

1. Charles Swindoll, *The Tale of the Tardy Oxcart* (Nashville, TN: Word Publishing, 1998), 322.

Postscript

1. I am aware that this last phrase, which I'm referring to as the seventh key, was likely added centuries later. But it is a good policy.

HOW TO CONTACT
EDDIE AND ALICE SMITH

Author, speaker, preacher Eddie Smith, and his wife, Alice, travel worldwide teaching on various themes related to prayer and discipleship.

The Smiths teach together as well as individually.

For information about hosting the Smiths for a conference in your church or city, submit your online invitation at: *www.usprayercenter.org*.

Prayer Resources

Eddie and Alice Smith's books and materials, as well as other resources they recommend, can be found at: *www.prayerbookstore.com*.

Free Newsletter

Join thousands worldwide who receive the PrayerNet Newsletter, Eddie and Alice's FREE biweekly informative e-mail publication. Subscribe at: *www.usprayercenter.org*.

Eddie Smith
U.S. PRAYER CENTER
7710-T Cherry Park Dr., Ste. 224
Houston, TX 77095
Phone: (713) 466-4009, (800) 569-4825 (U.S. only)
FAX: (713) 466-5633
E-mail: usprayercenter@cs.com
Web site: *www.usprayercenter.org*
Resource Center: *www.prayerbookstore.com*

More Spiritual Insight from Eddie and Alice Smith

PRAY MORE STRATEGICALLY AND EFFECTIVELY

Prayer practitioners Eddie Smith and Michael L. Hennen identify important principles that will equip you to pray more purposefully and effectively. Using them, you will learn the enemy's goals and strategies and prepare for victory as God's glory is revealed. Spiritual mapping tools are also given to enhance both personal and corporate prayer. This goal-based, proactive approach to prayer will bring results in individuals, churches, cities, and nations as you enter into partnership with God.

Strategic Prayer by Eddie Smith and Michael L. Hennen

ARE YOU SAVED BUT NOT FREE?

In straightforward, easy to understand teaching, Eddie Smith takes you through a step-by-step process that will set you free from the wounds and hurts of the past, including unforgiveness, sinful habits, occult activity, and self-condemnation. You'll discover how to identify areas of bondage, break contracts with the enemy, and cleanse close the wound, and much more. Follow the steps to spiritual freedom and you'll experience the victory Christ died to give you.

Breaking the Enemy's Grip by Eddie Smith

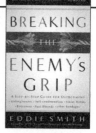

CLAIM YOUR FREEDOM IN CHRIST

Drawing on her careful study of Scripture and her thirty-five years of delivering Christians from spiritual oppression, Alice Smith shows how people struggling with strongholds can claim lasting victory. Here she offers the keys to unlocking lives from the bonds of depression, witchcraft, fear, victimization, and more. Also included is Alice's much sought-after list of Apparent Demonic Groupings as well as prayers, proclamations, and pronouncements to help readers rid themselves of evil in their lives and the lives of others.

Delivering the Captives by Alice Smith

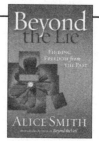

THROWING OFF THE LIES THAT HOLD US BACK

We all have struggles and difficulties in our lives—and often- times we fall prey to the lie that we aren't strong enough or good enough to be rid of them. We can feel trapped in our own unworthiness, allowing sin a stronger, deeper grip. Through her testimony, Alice Smith paints a powerful and practical picture of how you can overcome even the most deeply rooted sins and struggles. Her story is one of God's deliverance and grace—and yours can be as well.

Beyond the Lie by Alice Smith